People assume that the CEO of an organizing company and author of several organizing books is a "naturally organized" person...

...Nothing could be further from the truth! I am a living example that organizing skills can be learned. My organizing skills are a gift from my parents which have totally impacted my personal life, my career, the organizing industry, and the clients we serve. If you choose to accept this gift from Debbie, your life and the lives of the people around you, will be ultimately richer.

Barbara Hemphill
Author of Kiplinger's *Taming the Paper Tiger at Home*

"Have you recently tripped through a child's room, littered with toys and clothes, searching for the sports permission form that was due yesterday? Then you and your child NEED Debbie's new book, *Organized Kidz*. Whether you just need a little nudge to get started or a major overhaul on your lives, Debbie's book has ideas and strategies to help parents help their children finally get organized. Help is here!"

Christine Field
Author of *Life Skills for Kids*, *Help for the Harried Homeschooler*, *Homeschooling the Challenging Child*

"This book covers every—and I mean every—area of organization that would concern a child or parent. And unlike many books, it is written to speak directly to the kid—in an intelligent and articulate manner that doesn't patronize older children and teens."

Ramona Creel
Founder of OnlineOrganizing.com

ORGANIZED KIDZ

E-Z Solutions for Clutter-Free Living

by Debbie and David Williams

By the Book Media
Houston, Texas

BY THE BOOK MEDIA
HOUSTON, TX
Copyright © 2005 Debbie and David Williams

Cover & Interior Design by Donna Murphy
Edited by Donna Murphy
Back cover photo provided by Barry Williams

Cover photos provided by Lillian Vernon Corporation, Box4Blox™ and UniKeep™.
uniKeep™ is a trademark of uniKeep LLC. Used with permission.

ISBN: 0972698337
Printed in the United States of America

Contents

Section 1
Conquer that Clutter

Section 2
Time Management for Busy Kids

Section 3
Follow That Paper Trail

Chapter 3
Thanks for the Memories **97**

Section 4
Closing Thoughts

Appendix
Useful Tools for Kids and Their Families

Acknowledgments

I'd like to thank my son David, without him this book would not have been possible. His persistent dream of working together on a book for kids has finally come true.

Many thanks go to our production team: Donna Murphy, whose artistic gifts never cease to amaze me, and my dear friends Brenda Tigges and Kelly Schumann for their encouragement. Thanks for your prayers, support, and for letting us test our ideas on you and your children.

Thanks so much to all the homeschooling moms who participated in our *Organized Kidz* Survey. Your willingness to go the extra mile to help an author with research is much appreciated, and I couldn't have completed this book without you.

Most of all, we'd both like to thank God with whom all things are possible!

Introduction

As parents, it's our responsibility to love and nurture our children, to teach them right from wrong, and to protect them from the harsh world outside of our cozy family circle. Too often we do this to a fault. We nurture and protect without showing them how to fend for themselves.

Maybe we should look around and take our cues from nature. Mother birds lay their eggs, keep them warm, and then one day out hatches a baby bird that's brand new to the world around it. Does that mama bird encourage her babies to stay near the nest to keep her company in her old age, or does she nudge them to the edge to take that leap of faith that results in independent flight?

Now I'm not saying we should give birth and then turn our children loose outside in diapers to become free spirits! We have been given stewardship of these young people, and it's our ultimate responsibility to teach them how to be the very best they can possibly be. Let's make sure that they can fend for themselves after they leave the nest.

Many of the parents I consult with are so tired of *doing* and are ready for living. They've sacrificed for their kids so that their kids would have a better life than they did. Little Matthew is enrolled in sports every season, plus lessons for trombone and chess. Ashley is taking piano, tennis, and plays in the symphony. And little Tonya has to do her homework in the car while riding with mom from one activity to the next. Who has time for studying, much less cleaning their room?

**And then there's the clutter. Let's talk about the clutter!
I think we can all relate to this picture.**

Now I'm not living the simple life in a cave without electricity, and I sure don't expect you to either. But it sure seems like common sense that if you can't easily organize all your stuff, then maybe you should get rid of some of it. Being married to a packrat for over twenty years has really opened my eyes to those who suffer from "Packrat Syndrome," so I really do feel your pain.

Whether you're a packrat (I mean, *collector*) or just live with one, it's challenging to contain the clutter and keep it from overtaking your home. But if you're allowing more stuff to come into your home in order to live the good life, or worse yet, to keep up with friends or neighbors, then what kind of lesson are you teaching your children? What values are they learning from you, as they watch you go into debt each Christmas "maxing out" your credit cards?

I want to encourage you to teach your children one of the best life skills they can possibly learn: the gift of organization. No, I don't mean you need to buy a gift certificate from The Container Store® or purchase stock in Rubbermaid®! Just teach them how to organize their lives by conquering everyday clutter and managing their time.

My son David is a packrat, just like his dad. He loves to collect all kinds of stuff, from flashlights to rocks and broken cell phones. It's no easy feat organizing his room when it's full of broken toys and electronic parts lying all over the floor. Add to this mixture a packrat father who likes to take him garage sale shopping, and you have the formula for clutter overload.

My job as a mom, especially one who has a passion for organization, is to provide David with the skills he needs to succeed in life. I want him to set limits and have boundaries on his purchases, and resist bringing lots of unnecessary stuff into our home. It's a constant struggle for us all, but we've managed to implement a few household rules to contain the collections and keep things under control. The "one in, one out" rule works well, as does the "quarterly purge". (You'll learn more about these rules later in this book, but for now, just know that this mom is hunkered down in the trenches with you, struggling to reclaim her household one room at a time.)

David has wanted to share our household organizing strategies with others for some time now, but I've been busy with other projects so his idea has stayed on the back burner. Over the years, he's observed how disorganization can affect others. So now he is passionate about teaching common sense organizing skills to other families—to help them eliminate the stress and chaos in their lives, too.

Our desire for you is that your children will learn simple yet effective ways to manage their time, clear and maintain the clutter, and work together at home so that no one feels they are the only clutterbug in the bunch. They'll learn how to organize any space in four steps and discover better ways to manage their schedules. They'll also create a file system of their own to keep those pesky papers under control, too.

We've written this book to be read by young people and parents together. However, older kids may want to read the book, and then sit down and plan out their organizing strategies with mom or dad. Early readers can read the tips and sidebars while working through the activities with their parents. For children younger than age eight, we recommend that the parents read the book to them and then implement a few of the activities with their children, or they can pitch in to help older siblings get their stuff in order.

Regardless of your level of organization (or lack thereof), we hope that you'll find comfort and encouragement as you work together through the clutter in your busy lives. Think of organizing as a journey, not a destination, and this book is your roadmap to a happy, stress-free trip. Happy organizing!

Debbie and David Williams
August 2005

SECTION 1

Conquer that Clutter

CHAPTER 1
How to Become an
Awesome Organizer

Getting organized is as simple as 1, 2, 3 and 4. In my experience working with people of all ages, from moms and dads to teenagers, this simple 4-step process has worked wonders in creating a manageable organizing system. It's one that you'll continue to use at home, school, and even in the backseat of your family's car!

PLAN for success

SORT through your clutter

ORGANIZE what's left

MAINTAIN your system each day

Step 1: Plan for Success

Write It Down

Lights, Camera, Action! Before you plunge in over your head with your organizing project, you need to create an Action Plan. Whether you use an Action Plan form like the one in this book, a notebook, or a journal, it's important to start with a place to make notes and track your progress. It doesn't have to be fancy. Just make it easy to use, and keep it close so you can find it when you need it.

Identify Your Clutter Zones

Use a toy telescope or an empty paper towel tube to get a realistic view of your clutter. Walk around your room looking through the telescope to get tunnel vision of the actual clutter in your space. This is one time it's okay *not* to look at your whole room. Just zoom in on *one* little area of your most cluttered space, and begin your journey there. Isn't it amazing how looking through this little scope helps you zoom in on the clutter zone?

From Dream to Reality

Whether it's your closet, playroom, or desk, focus on a small space and then form a picture in your mind of how you would *like* for it to look. Would you like to see that pile of clothes on the floor disappear and be neatly organized in your closet instead? Maybe you have the dream of an organized

3

area for all your sports equipment. Take a few minutes to draw a picture of what you would like for your space to look like. You don't have to be a great artist to do this. Just draw shelves, boxes, racks, or tubs to hold your gear and collections. Use your favorite colors and don't forget to leave plenty of room for just hanging out with your friends. Very soon you'll see that huge monstrous pile dwindle down to a little collection of stuff that is just waiting to be organized. Oops! I'm getting ahead of myself…That's not part of the planning step, but we'll get to the organizing stage soon, I promise!

✋ Hands-On Time: Plan for Success

Take a moment to list your biggest problem area in the worksheet provided at right. Focus on the one area that is the absolutely the worst clutter zone, and then we'll tackle the rest at another time. First things first!

> *The secret of getting ahead is getting started. The secret of getting started is breaking your complex overwhelming tasks into small manageable tasks, and then starting on the first one.*
>
> *~ Mark Twain*

My Biggest Problem Area:

_____

_____

_____

Grab your Action Plan and write down the biggest organized dream you have for your new space.

- **How would you like for it to look every day?**

- **What things will you store there?**

- **What activities will you be doing there?**

- **What kinds of equipment or containers will you need to make this dream come true?**

Write those down in the lines below.

My Biggest Dream for Organizing This Space:

_____

_____

_____

_____

_____

_____

_____

_____

Are you ready to sort through the clutter now? Hang on, we're almost ready! The planning step is the most important step of all. Wait a little bit longer as we take the time to create one last part of your Action Plan—and then you'll be able to grab those containers and fill them up to your heart's content. I promise it'll be worth the wait!

Now it's time for action! Create an Action Plan by listing all the problem areas of your room on a large sheet of paper. For example, you might list: closet, desk, sports gear in the garage, your bathroom, and so forth. Choose the one that you would like to begin with first and then put the number "1" beside it. Find the second biggest organizing challenge and place a "2" beside it. Continue this *prioritizing* step until you have assigned a number to each room you have selected.

Make an Appointment

Set a deadline to organize your room and mark that date on your planning sheet. Don't just guess. Grab a calendar and make a big effort to really reach your deadline. Check off each area as it is completed and include that date in your notes. This will be a guide for future projects.

Step 2: Sort Through the Clutter

Now that you've created a plan for action, it's time to start **sorting**. Tackle one area at a time—and don't worry; the rest of the clutter will still be there when you're ready to conquer it!

 Did You Know?

prioritizing: sorting in order by putting the more important things first and the less important things last.

sorting: grouping things together that are the same.

Create sorting labels for your stacks by writing each of these words on a piece of notebook paper: TRASH, KEEP, SELL/GIVE AWAY, UNDECIDED. (Notebook paper will work just fine, or you can add color to your work by using construction paper for your sorting signs.)

Set up sturdy and easy-to-use sorting boxes for your organizing project, one for each of the four categories that I listed above.

You might want to use cardboard boxes from your neighborhood grocery store, or have your mom or dad buy some banker's boxes from the office supply store that can be used over and over again. Your boxes don't have to be fancy, but they should be sturdy enough that they don't fall apart. Tape the labels onto your boxes instead of gluing them so you can easily remove the labels to be used another time.

Sort First, Organize Later

Begin this step of the organizing process by sorting the items in your cluttered little corner of the world. (Remember your #1 Problem Area? That's where we'll start.) Pick up and take action on one piece at a time, working around the room until you've sorted through everything in your clutter zone. You can go in a circle or zigzag pattern—whatever feels most natural to you.

Remember to sort first, and then worry later about the storage and organization steps. Try not to get too attached to anything you pick up during this step. Later, during your break, you can look through your scattered stacks of pictures and trophies, but right now it's time for action! Sorting is one of my personal favorites of the four organizing steps, because it's so easy. Anyone can sort socks, shoes, shirts, papers, and toys, grouping like things together and tossing them into the appropriate boxes.

Remember when you were in preschool and learned that some things belong together, and others don't? That's sorting at its most basic level. Just think, you've been doing it all along and didn't even know it. You're going to be really good at this!

Ask your mom or dad to help you, or invite a friend to join in the sorting party. Listen to your favorite music to keep you moving. But don't leave your sorting area to put things away, because you'll probably get sidetracked down the hall or in the garage and forget to return to where you first began. I call this puddle jumping, because it's like jumping from one area to the other, and doesn't really get you anywhere. Try to stay on course!

What to Do with All that Stuff?

Before you can take the next step, you must do something with all that stuff you've sorted. Let's start with the easiest stack, and then work our way up to the hardest (which is another good time management tip).

If you have any questions about whether or not to throw something away, check with your parents first. Sometimes they're able to fix something that seems beyond help, and maybe your favorite flashlight or best pair of jeans can become as good as new after they work their parental skills on it. Or perhaps those jeans that are too tight for you can be saved for your little sister to wear when she's older. So when in doubt, ask.

> *Never put off till tomorrow*
> *what you can do today.*
>
> *~ Thomas Jefferson*

Take a time-out to carry the TRASH box outside to your garbage can, dumpster or to the curb for pick up. Go ahead and remove it from the room so that you don't have to deal with it taking up valuable space. Wow, that part was easy, wasn't it?

Now it's time to move to the SELL or GIVE AWAY box. Carry it to your mom or dad's car to drop off tomorrow at a charity or resell shop. If it's filled with clothes and shoes to hand down to your sisters and brothers, you'll need to ask your parents where to store it. They probably have a good system in place for this already and can show you where it belongs, probably in the attic or under their bed in a storage box.

Let's take another look at that UNDECIDED box—you know, the one with the great big question mark on it? When you've gotten this far in the sorting process, it's a lot easier to toss out things that you would normally keep. If anything is left in the box, move it to the hallway for now. You can always tackle it after your break. See? This won't be too bad. We're only on Step 2 and you're already getting a break!

That leaves you with the KEEP box, which is the only box of stuff you will actually be organizing today. It's finally time to use all those shoeboxes, milk crates, and tackle boxes that you've been saving in the bottom of your closet!

Step 3: Organize What's Left

It's time to get organized! At last, it's time to finally **organize** all that stuff you've sorted through. Use containers from your closet and garage to contain the clutter you've sorted, and remember that the items used the most should be easiest to access. Things that you don't use very often can be boxed up, labeled, and stored in the attic or basement.

If you've done your homework correctly (that is moving from Step 1 to Step 2 without skipping ahead to Step 3), your organizing job won't be nearly as hard as you thought it would be. This is where you will make a home for your treasured items to live so that you can find them whenever you need them.

To keep track of your stuff, create *zones* or centers, just like you had in kindergarten. Use common sense to set up the zones in your bedroom, bathroom, or garage. Store clothes in drawers or hang in your closet, set sports gear on racks or shelves, stash crafts supplies in drawers and bins, and display computer games on your desk. Really there's no wrong way to do this, just whatever makes sense to *you* (and wherever you will look for things when you need to use them later).

> *Half our life is spent trying to find something to do with the time we have rushed through life trying to save.*
>
> ~ Will Rogers

👋 Hands-On Time: Around the House

Imagine yourself using these things in your room. On any given day, think about how and where you would use them. For example, if you're a **kinesthetic learner** (that means that you learn by doing, not just seeing or hearing), and you need to write things down to make sense of your thoughts, use the space below to make some notes.

Storage Notes:

_____

_____

_____

_____

_____

Most kids stuff their sports gear in their room after a game or toss them into the coat closet, and then they can't find it all when they need it. But what if you stored your baseball, bat, glove, uniform and shoes in your bedroom closet where you could find them fast? What if your favorite belt was near your pants instead of halfway across the room under your bed?

By thinking clearly about where items are actually used, rather than stuffing them into leftover storage space, you're making a home and establishing a good habit. Now

each time you finish using your cleats, you'll know where to return them and anyone else in the house can find them, too.

Use this same exercise with the rest of the stuff in your KEEP stack if they become a storage challenge. It's okay to think outside the box (that means creatively thinking), and to store things in other rooms, especially if you share them with other people in your family. Maybe you share markers with your sister and they need to be stored in the kitchen drawer. Or your brother plays the same video game that you do, so you should keep the disc in the family room so that you both can find it fast. Not everything that you keep will stay in your room, but it's a good place to start.

Step 4: Maintain Your System Every Day

Keep up the hard work by **maintaining** your new organizing system. This seems to be the most challenging and overlooked step in organizing. It's pretty easy to *get* organized, but how on earth do you *stay* that way? Remember all those creative ideas you came up with in the organizing step of your project? All those file boxes, binders, and storage boxes that you wanted to use? They helped you to create a home for your papers and treasures, and that's where you should keep storing things on a regular basis.

Don't let this organizing step overwhelm you. It's simply a matter of cleaning as you

JUST ANOTHER NORMAL DAY

The alarm clock wakes you to music that helps you start your day with a smile. You walk to the bathroom and brush your teeth while waiting for the shower to warm up. After your shower, you realize that you've used the last of the toothpaste, so you make a note on Mom's Inventory Sheet hanging inside your linen closet door so that she can buy you more. (AND if Mom doesn't use inventory sheets, you remind yourself to mention it later at breakfast.)

As you hang up your wet towel, you realize that you have a spelling test later today. It's such a relief that you did your homework last night and put it away in your backpack with your student planner. Of course choosing what to wear today is a breeze since clothes have been laid out for the entire week in your closet.

Walking into the kitchen, you see your family gathered around the table because their clothes were cleaned, pressed and lined up in the closet at the beginning of the week, too. Now everyone can sit down and enjoy a calm and nutritious breakfast—no more bites on the run for this organized family!

Since lunches were prepared last night, you can grab yours from the fridge and put it into your backpack with your completed homework hanging on the rack by the door. Mom can return that new video you watched after school on her way to work because you put it in her tote bag last night.

You and your family are up, dressed, and prepared to start your day in an orderly (and joyful) manner. Wow! You might even have time for a glance at your student planner to see what's on the agenda today.

go, and taking the time to put things back where they belong after you use them.

Ah, the Possibilities!

Some organizing experts feel that there must be a place for everything, and everything should be in its place. But that would be in a perfect world, wouldn't it? My room certainly isn't perfect, and I'll bet yours isn't either! Instead of giving up before we even get started, let's pretend to take a walk through your normal day and its wonderfully organized possibilities.

This may seem almost like a fairy tale, but so many parts of this scene can be played out in your own home if you use the organizing steps outlined in this book. How about it? Let's get busy making your dream come true!

 **Dave SayZ ...**

Cleaning up your toys every day is better than cleaning up your toys once a week. That way it doesn't keep piling up.

Keeping it Simple

Use common sense organizing techniques to keep your space simple. Don't be afraid to reorganize or move items around as things change. Thinking *in the zone* helps you with the long-term plan of getting your space in order, making room for playing, studying, hanging out with your friends, and sleeping. I think that since these are action words, we may as well call your task centers *action zones*.

In the next chapter, we'll learn how to set up action zones in your living space, room by room. You'll learn about four options for organizing all your stuff, and how to organize things in your bedroom, family room, basement or garage, and even in the car. What are you waiting for? Let's get organized!

> *Our life is frittered away by detail ... Simplify, Simplify.*
>
> *~ Henry David Thoreau*

Chapter Notes

Chapter Notes

Chapter Notes

CHAPTER 2
Room by Room

Organize your space by practicing these **Four Basic Solutions for Storage:**

1. **Hang it**

2. **Put it in a drawer**

3. **Store it on the floor**

4. **Shelve it**

If you use these four simple strategies, you can easily contain the clutter in a closet, garage, basement, bathroom, bedroom or playroom. The concepts are the same no matter what area you're trying to de-clutter, and the containers don't need to be fancy either. You can hang a bathroom towel on a wooden hat rack from the dollar store, or invest in an expensive over-the-door rack from an upscale home improvement store; it just depends on your budget and the available resources. But the results will be the same: the clutter is off the floor and out of the way. It now has a new home to go to each and every day.

Begin to tackle your problem areas, one room at a time, until all the spaces in your life are not only orderly, but easy to manage.

The Bathroom

Surviving the morning rush in any busy household isn't easy, especially if you and your family are sharing bathroom space. Organizing small spaces can easily reduce bathroom clutter. Use **vertical space** whenever you can, cut down on using lots of towels, and create a place for all those dirty clothes to reduce the bathroom clutter in

---

? **Did You Know?**

vertical organizing: storing stuff up and down in shelves or bookcases instead of stacking them on tables or the floor. **?**

---

your home. Here are a few ideas to get you started. Of course, you don't have to use all of them; just choose your favorites and get the rest of your family to join in as you create your new system.

What's Your Bag?

Use a basket, over-the-door laundry bag, or a bag that hangs on the doorknob to hold the clothes you normally would toss onto the floor.

Throw In the Towel

Assign each member of your family a colored towel to be used more than once. Choose a color and stick with it. Your towel might be blue, your sister's pink, your mom's red, and your dad's brown. (Hint: If the thought of reusing a towel again gives you the creeps, at least use the same clean towel again and again to dry your hair.)

Hang On

Hang towels on hooks, pegs, or over-the-door racks to take up less space. Most homes only have one or two towel racks and that's just not enough to hold all those damp towels that you use between wash loads.

Toss & Carry

For clothes that aren't ready for the laundry yet, start using the "toss-n-carry rule": if you toss it, you need to carry it back to your closet.

Tween Rack™

Hang a shaker peg or expandable hat rack in closets or on the door to hold those clothes that are *in between* dirty and clean. This works great for gym clothes, play clothes that you change into after school, or church clothes that you've only worn an hour or two.

Going Up!

Use stacking bins, over-the-toilet shelves, hanging wire baskets or other stacking containers for the stuff in your shared bathroom space. This works great for shampoos, brushes, hair scrunchies, toothpaste, dental floss, and other small things.

Group similar stuff together (like towels, wash cloths, or shampoo), or assign one shelf or basket for each family member. Your little sister's basket would be the lowest, yours might be in the middle, and Dad's might be on the top level. If you do use a hanging wire basket, try placing a cloth napkin or a strong paper towel in the bottom to keep those small things from falling through.

This Is a Stick Up

Use suction cups or adhesive tape to attach toothbrush holders, soap dishes, shampoo dispensers, and other bathroom organizers. But be sure to ask your mom or dad first, just in case it might leave a mark that you can't remove later. Or use a removable hook that is safe for any wall or cabinet.

Your Bedroom

It's finally time to create a private space of your own: your bedroom. Remember the Action Zones we talked about earlier? I know this sounds silly, but trust me on this one, okay? I'm a grown-up and I have a house full of zones, one for each activity in my day. Here are a few ideas to get you started:

- **Sleeping Zone** — bed, pillow, nightlight, stuffed animals.

- **Music Zone** — radio, cassettes or CDs, headphones, battery charger.

- **Video Zone** — beanbag chair or overstuffed bed pillow, remote controls, VHS tapes, tape organizer.

- **Computer Zone** — sturdy table, comfortable chair, foot rest, mouse pad, games and educational software, a shelf.

- **Homework Zone** — chair, table or desk, lamp, pencil, paper, research materials.

- **Reading Zone** — cozy chair, floor cushion, or beanbag; floor or desk lamp.

- **Housekeeping Zone** — table, chairs, kitchen, dishes, play food, vacuum or broom, different props for creative play for little girls and boys.

- **Drama Zone** — dress-up clothes on hooks or in a box, mirror, puppets.

- **DiscoveryZone** — aquarium or terrarium for fish/turtle/lizard, pet food, shelf or small table for collections, microscope, telescope, binoculars, flashlight, compass, magnet, magnifying glass.

- **Block Zone** — a place to build block towers and cities, maybe with carpet to keep things quiet, different sizes and shapes of blocks in wood, plastic or sturdy cardboard.

- **Carpet Zone** — plenty of floor space to play with dolls, cars, or action figures.

 Dave SayZ...

Reorganize your room once a month by sorting the things you want from the things you don't want.

Make sure that you get a good night's sleep by getting rid of the clutter in your bedroom. Try not to do too many big projects in your bedroom, and don't use your room as a storage area for things that belong in the pantry or basement. That means if you're working on a science project or you share a computer with your sister, you need to organize your workspace so that there isn't a lot of stuff out in plain sight.

Sometimes you can disguise it a bit by storing it in containers or by putting it behind a folding screen or closet doors. Here are some tips to help you get started:

- **Stash It** — Use flat storage tubs that store under the bed for clothes that you've outgrown, school papers, a model train set, or extra stuffed animals.

Be sure to use durable plastic tubs for long lasting storage. Also, label the ends of the boxes so you can find your neatly organized stuff the next time you need it!

- **Behind Closed Doors** — If your parents give you a budget, try to find a small cabinet with doors to use as a home computer station, or a wardrobe to hide your television and VCR.

Sometimes you can add shelves to a small closet and get the same results. Or be creative and hang a piece of canvas with Velcro® to create a curtain. Be sure to ask your parents first so that you don't ruin a perfectly good bookcase with Velcro® tape!

- **Under the Mattress** — If your linen closet is small or your house doesn't have one, try keeping a spare set of sheets tucked between your mattress and box springs; not only does this save space, but it saves time, too.

Now there's no need to run to another room for clean sheets when it's laundry day.

- **Instant Work Station** — Store a piece of ply board under your bed to use as a work surface for hobbies.

Laid flat on your mattress, it makes a wonderful surface for painting models, cutting foam board for science projects, or making posters for school. Then when it's time for sleep, just slip it under the bed, adjust the bed skirt, and your work will be out of sight.

Using this idea in a guest room can make double duty of the bedroom (that means it can do more than one thing). When you don't have company, you can turn the room into a hobby area for special projects. You can also quickly change it back to a bedroom again when Grandma comes for a visit.

Family Room

Use some of these creative solutions to organize and hide the clutter that is often created in the family room.

Screening Room: A freestanding screen can be bought from an import store, or found at a garage sale. Use a screen to hide playroom toys, crafts, model trains, or science projects.

Round it Up: Gather up loose objects, such as pens and paper, and store them inside a decorative box. Wooden cigar boxes, painted containers, or wicker baskets can easily contain tabletop clutter on your desk or nightstand.

Basket Case: Use baskets and crates in different sizes and shapes to hold action figures, magazines, and stuff to be put away in another room. Crates or cubes can easily stack to create a simple activity center, and they are easy to move around.

The Garage

Whether your family has a three-car garage or needs to store tools inside the kitchen cupboard, **garage clutter** really does affect us all. From attic to basement and beyond, no one is free from the challenge of wondering where to stash glues and wood-burning tools. Using the same organizing tips in the garage, as you do in the bathroom, will contain the clutter and keep you from searching everywhere when you need to work on a special project for scouts or school.

• Ask your mom or dad to hang thin wooden strips horizontally around the inside walls of your garage. Add large nails or hooks, and ta-da! You have an instant and inexpensive way to organize hockey sticks, skis, or kites.

Special NeedZ ...

Make a home for your books, medical records, and schedule. Keep all of your paperwork in one place such as a hanging file system or binder with pocketed folders. When it's time to report to your child's medical team, all your information is in one place.

• Use bike hooks to hang your cycles from the ceiling and get them out of the way. Some bike racks even lean against the wall and stack two bikes high, which is much easier to access. Others hang up high but work on a pulley system to raise and lower your bike only when you need it. Don't be afraid to ask for help with this. Mom will love having more space to park her van, and Dad will have more room for his workbench, too.

• Mount a large pegboard on the wall, add hooks, and you're ready for any handy project. Of course, you'll need help with this project, but it's a great one to do with your dad or uncle on a Saturday afternoon. Be sure to leave about ¼ inch between the board and the wall so that the hooks can grip the peg hole.

• Old kitchen cupboards and countertops make excellent garage organizers and they're usually free for the taking. If someone you know is remodeling their kitchen, just ask them if it's okay to take their old cabinets. Of course you want to get permission from your parents first, just in case they have another idea for organizing the garage space.

• Screw jar lids underneath garage shelves or cabinets, and then screw in the matching jar for instant and clutter-free organizers. Be sure to use plastic jars instead of glass ones for garage safety. If your family eats peanut butter as much as ours does,

you'll have an entire row of jars for your garage in no time!

• Store rolls of tape, coils of wire, and screws in wide-mouthed tubs and coffee cans. Tubs that once held margarine or ice cream are perfect containers for all kinds of things, and you can label them with a permanent marker so that you know what's inside.

• Turn over a tall stool to hold sporting goods such as hockey sticks, skis, fishing poles and baseball bats.

👋 Hands-On Time: Creative Organizing 101

Okay. Let's see how much you've learned about organizing. In the blanks on the next page provided for each product, I'd like for you to list *three creative ways* these items can be used to store the stuff in your house. Here's a hint: most of the answers are contained in the earlier chapters of this book, while others are inspired by organizing tips you've just learned.

I've done the first one for you, using ideas that I use in my own home. Suggestions can be found in the back of this book, but **there are no right or wrong answers**. Just use your imagination and you'll easily come up with some great ways to collect and store the clutter in your room and beyond!

Tiered Vegetable Basket
  art supplies   hair scrunchies   video game cases

Wooden Cigar Box

Film Canister

Makeup Bag

Zippered Pencil Case

3-Ring Notebook

Dishwashing Tub

Plastic Coat Hanger

Plastic Milk Crate

Wooden Peg Rack

Plastic Shoe Shelf

Canvas Book Bag

Chapter Notes

Chapter Notes

Chapter Notes

CHAPTER 3
In the Zone

Boxes, Bins and Tubs

Remember all of those plastic tubs with lids that Mom bought on sale to help you get organized? You know the ones, stacked in your closet or the garage floor? Well, now is the perfect time to put them to use.

Blocks, doll clothes, Legos®, small toy cars, Tinkertoys®, Playdoh®, and all the other loose things floating around the house belong together. I strongly recommend using shelves with tubs of different sizes instead of toy boxes. Toys last much longer when they're stored gently and not stacked, and you can also find things easier when they're displayed rather than in a jumbled stack.

Small plastic shoeboxes are ideal for storing Legos®, Barbie® accessories, and Hot Wheels®. Use totes a size larger with handles on the top for easy carrying to and from the play area. Larger tubs hold blocks, tea sets, dishes, and other pieces that just seem to multiply in the night. Save those extra-large tubs for train sets, car tracks, doll accessories, and sports gear.

Flat under-the-bed boxes are wonderful for extra clothes and toys. Most closets are just not large enough for both toys and clothes, so why not store unused toys as you would store your clothing? Kites, beach gear, and baseball equipment can be stashed during winter months; football, hockey stick, and ice skates are stored during the summertime.

 **Dave SayZ ...**

Use bins with handles on the lids to separate your stuff into categories. That way you know where everything is, and you can easily take it with you.

Try to buy clear see-through tubs, or label them with words or pictures. If you can't see what's inside, chances are you won't use the toys in the newly organized containers either! (Defeats the purpose for putting them in containers, don't you think?)

Get creative, and maybe even let your younger sisters or brothers help you label the boxes with pictures, stickers, or magazine clippings of the items. It's a good rainy day project, and promotes reading skills for the little ones, too. (Shh, don't tell them that they're learning something new!)

Vertical Storage

One of the key rules of organizing and decorating is to use as much **vertical space** as you can in a room. Usually we place furniture around the room with nothing above it, forming a nice horizontal line (that's low to the ground and around the room). But there is a ton of unclaimed storage and attractive space living right above the furniture line!

Hat racks, whether they expand or have sturdy pegs for hanging, make wonderful holders for stuffed animals, dress-up clothes, jackets, backpacks, and book bags.

Smaller items can be hung and grouped by function (how you use them): sports gear (baseball hat, glove, cleats), or fashion (jewelry, belts, scarves, hats**).**

Did You Know?

vertical organizing: storing stuff up and down in shelves or bookcases instead of stacking them on tables or the floor.

Most kids find something they like and want lots of it. But is more really better? I once saw an entire wall of a kids' room lined with pegged hat racks, creating a chair rail. The pegs were at eye level for toddlers and waist level for older kids, who hung stuffed animals, hats, totes filled with blocks, and other lightweight treasures. This is another great example of creative organizing.

To further use vertical space, have your mom or dad install wooden shelves and paint them to match the color on your walls. Hang toy hammocks for your collection of stuffed animals. Spray paint a shower rod, wrap it with strips of Velcro®, and stick on your stuffed animals. Now you have room on your bed for rest where there once was a zoo!

The 3-Toy Rule

In the early grades of elementary school (kindergarten through third grade), classrooms are set up in learning centers. And to contain the clutter in the classroom, teachers usually have a rule of putting a toy away *before* taking out another one. This may seem extreme in your home and may not work well, but it's certainly worth a try.

Now when my own son David was younger, we had a three-toy rule: he could play with up to three toys, and then he had to put them away before dragging out another one. The rule works well with things such as puzzles, books and blocks. But be sure to allow plenty of shelves and containers for this system.

I discovered when my son was a baby that his board books fell right through the slatted bookcase in his room, so I bought stacking bins in bright colors for the smaller books. We used the bookcase for large toys and tubs of smaller toys instead. If you start using this rule when you're younger, it helps you establish a **Clean As You Go Habit** throughout your life. (You'll hear me talk a lot about this rule. It's my favorite!)

Inside or Out?

How many times have you heard Mom say, "Come in or stay out, but please make up your mind"? In Texas where we live, if you leave the door open too long, the flies come in and the cool air rushes right out. Toys in the hands of an active kid follow the same path. It's important to make sure at the end of the day that baseball mitts are not left outside, and bubble mowers are not dripping onto the family room carpet.

Assign rules to the toys and try to stick to them, such as: inside toys, outside toys, upstairs toys, and downstairs toys. Sometimes this is a safety rule, such as any toy that can be thrown should be played with OUTDOORS (like balls, bats, Frisbeesâ). All things made of paper are kept INDOORS (such as books, kites, journals).

This rule was created from a little common sense and a lot of experience. We've all left out a favorite book outside that has gotten wet overnight from the dew. Likewise, some of us have accidentally broken a lamp by tossing a football in the family room. Yikes! Maybe with some smart planning, we can prevent this from happening in your household.

Upstairs or Down?

If you live in a two-story home, upstairs toys shouldn't be dragged down the stairs, but should stay in your bedroom or the playroom instead. Keep a few toys on a small shelf, in a wicker basket or toy bin

Finish each day and be done with it …
You have done what you could; some
blunders and absurdities no doubt crept
in; forget them as soon as you can.
Tomorrow is a new day; you shall begin
it well and serenely.

~ Ralph Waldo Emerson

downstairs in the family room, but tidy up each night before you go to bed.

Downstairs riding toys should stay downstairs and off the steps so that no one trips over them. (I realize you're too old for those riding toys, but your little sister or brother isn't, and you can help manage their clutter, too.)

Following Through

Old wooden soda crates found at a garage sale can be cleaned up and painted. Fill the crate with your treasures such as: shells, rocks, key rings and kids meal toys. Shadow boxes bought from craft stores make wonderful displays for ribbons, pins, and badges that you've worked so hard to earn. You know, experts in decorating encourage us to keep our collections, but to consolidate rather than scatter them for more drama. (That means grouping similar things together to make a bigger impact.)

Create a budget, make a list of things you need to store, and see what you can come up with. Perhaps you'll want to take a boxful to your favorite children's charity, or have a garage sale to raise money for that special toy you've been wanting for awhile. Getting involved in the planning, prioritizing, sorting, and containing stages guarantees better (but not perfect) maintenance of clutter. And who knows? You may actually

become a minimalist in the process (someone who has very few things in their home and likes a simple environment) or maybe just a packrat with very organized closets!

When you hear something, you will forget it.

When you see something, you will remember it.

But not until you do something will you understand it.

- ancient Chinese proverb

Chapter Notes

Chapter Notes

CHAPTER 4
Organizing On the Go

Now that we've organized your room and the shared spaces of your house, it's time to tackle those areas of your life that go with you: your backpack, school locker, and the family car. But don't get discouraged just yet. Organizing on the go is the same as organizing any other space. Just remember the four steps of Awesome Organizing™ (Plan, Sort, Organize and Maintain) and you'll be conquering the portable clutter in no time.

A Matter of Style

How many times have you gone on summer vacation with your family and run out of gas? Or gotten completely lost because you had no map to show you the way? Right! This doesn't happen too often does it? And although your family isn't perfectly organized all the time, at least your mom or dad tries to keep gas in the van, a map in the glove box, and has some sort of a plan to know where you're headed on your trip.

Your organizing journey should be designed in the same way: with a plan for where you're going and how you'll get there. There are many different ways to plan a vacation, from detailed schedules to just driving until you get tired and need to stop for rest. You can look at organizing your personal clutter in the same way, building a plan for success and setting things up in a way that is right for *you*.

For example, if you're one of those people who needs to have everything out so that you don't forget to use it, try storing your gear in clear zippered bags and containers. Or maybe you're a neat-freak and want everything lined up just so. Storing things in bins with compartments in your desk is a good fit for your organizing style.

Some people need to touch things to remind them to take action. If you are one of them, you'll need to hang onto original notes, cards, and papers to help you organize your schedule. File them into an organizer with pockets that has a secure flap or zipper so that your notes don't escape, Soon you'll be ready to get down to business!

Gathering Your Tools

Once you figure out your organizing style, it'll be time to plan what you will need to store in your locker or backpack. And then, of course, you'll need to figure out how to store it so you can find it later. Most department stores have some awesome organizers for students that are made with your needs in mind. There are plenty of pockets, files, and room for notes.

Think of your backpack as a suitcase with many different uses. Consider setting up compartments for each use, such as pencil bags for pencils and protractors, a makeup bag for comb and Chapstick®, and another small bag to store granola bars for those extra-long days when you'll need an energy boost.

Office supply stores sell locker organizers such as mirrors, shelves, pencil bags, magnetic clips, and memo boards for jotting down reminders. The best tip I can give you for organizing on the go is to avoid relying on your planner alone for all your organizing needs.

The notebook planner that your school gives to every student is a one-size-fits-all

tool, but it doesn't always work to your advantage or your organizing style. Not everyone learns (or organizes) in the same way, so it's okay to fill in the gaps with other types of organizers to help keep you on track.

Colorful Post-it notes® inside your locker door will remind you that Mom's picking you up early to leave for Grandma's this Friday. Mesh pencil bags inside your notebook can hold a reminder from your teacher that your English assignment is due next Wednesday. Pocketed folders are great for storing those reports in progress. Be creative and compare notes with your friends— you might learn a thing or two from them.

Tips for Organizing Car Clutter

So many of us spend a lot of time in our car, riding to school and back again, going to ball games, music lessons, and all the other activities in our busy lives. Books, backpacks, and sports gear seem to fly around in the back of Mom's minivan faster than we can catch them! But with a few simple tricks, you can contain car clutter and keep it from hiding under the seat or falling out the door.

Use some of the tips listed on the following pages to create a mini-filing system and organize all those items carried during outings.

> *When you get to the end of your rope,*
> *tie a knot and hang on.*
> *~ Franklin D. Roosevelt*

• What's Your Hang-up?

Store important papers in hanging files in a portable crate. These are available in different sizes, and are either open at the top or have sturdy lids to close them. To prevent the crate from sliding around while you're traveling, place a fluffy towel underneath the crate, or store it on the floorboard where it won't tip over.

It's a great way to organize school permission slips, work in progress, or notes from your teacher. (Be sure to keep your papers separate from your mom and dad's so there are no surprises when they get to work and conduct a business meeting with your history report!)

• Read Between The Lines

Carry a To Read folder with you for reading in the car or on the bus. This is a great time-saver and reduces stress, too.

• It's All In The System

Create a follow-up system using a notebook with pocketed dividers, a plastic recipe box or **accordion file** (accordion files are those expanding folders that have several dividers to keep your papers separated.).

Number the dividers 1-30, and file your assignments behind the correct date of the month for later action.

• What's On The Agenda?

Consolidate (gather together) all your important notes into a daily planner, spiral notebook, calendar, or small wipe-off board. If your family keeps a master-planning calendar at home, carry a portable spare in your car for making notes. Be sure to remember to update it with the master calendar each day to prevent overlooked appointments and those special days such as recitals and competitions.

• Go Mobile

For a desk-on-the-go, buy a 3-ring notebook and fill it with pocketed dividers; one for each subject at school plus your outside activities. Label each one with main headings such as: Science, Math, English, as well as after-school activities such as Sports, Music, and other important events.

Now you're ready to fill the pockets with all those important schedules, reading lists and report assignments. The binder can be used as a portable desk, or can be stored at school in your locker. Don't forget to stick your favorite writing pen into the front pocket so you'll always be prepared to update it.

• Improved Storage Space

Keep a large crate or laundry basket in your car to hold fund-raising products, uniforms, library books and rented videos. Or maybe splurge and have an extra one so that you can carry a full one into the house, saving wasted trips from the car to the kitchen. My all-time favorite is a collapsible plastic crate that doesn't take up much space when it's empty. We keep it in the back of our car to hold books, backpacks, packages, and containers of cupcakes for a party.

• It's The Little Things That Count

There are a number of visor and glove compartment organizers available that will neatly store your pens, paper, sunglasses, and lunch money. Make it a habit to put small objects away after you use them so you can easily find them just when you need them most.

• More Leg Room

Expand the limited floor space in your family car by using pocketed organizers that hang on the back of the car seat. These hold umbrellas, sunscreen, CD players, portable video games, and snacks for those long days away from home.

• A Compact Model

Create a small locker-on-the-go by filling a zippered pencil case with school supplies for your backpack, messenger bag, or car. Store basic desk drawer items such as: calculator, pads of paper, pens, pencils, stapler and staple remover, scissors, tape dispenser, Post-it® notes,

rubber bands, paper clips, and loose change.

• Emergency Road Care

Gather together first-aid supplies, a large towel or blanket, rain poncho, and a change of clothes. Store them in a tote bag, grocery sack, or old backpack. (Now if this sounds like someone's mother telling you to always be prepared, you're absolutely right! We parents realize the value of an emergency change of clothes for our kids no matter how old they are.)

Mini-kits such as the ones I've listed here come in all shapes and sizes, from school supplies to a change of clothes. Using everyday items to organize our backpacks and cars will not only help us do our best work, but will get rid of much of the stress we bump into along the way.

Are you ready to find more hours in your busy day? Great, let's keep going! You'll quickly learn the basics of **time management** so you can have more fun time together with your friends and family.

Chapter Notes

Chapter Notes

SECTION 2
Time Management for Busy Kids

CHAPTER 1
It's About Time

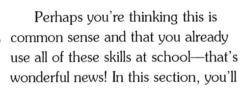

In this part of our organizing journey, we'll be discussing the Five Steps to Becoming a Successful Time Manager. The definition of a Time Manager is exactly what it sounds like: someone who can manage their time and get things done.

Perhaps you're thinking this is common sense and that you already use all of these skills at school—that's wonderful news! In this section, you'll learn practical ways to depend upon someone beside yourself to get all those important things done.

You'll be able to include the same time management tools that Mom and Dad use to manage your time at school and home. You'll learn how to:

- **PRIORITIZE** your tasks instead of just making a long list

- **DELEGATE** your work

- **LIMIT** interruptions

- **CONSOLIDATE** your tasks

- **USE TIME BLOCKS** for better organization

 **Dave SayZ ...**

Make a schedule for your day and stick to it so you'll remember what you need to do. Use either a notebook or a calendar.

Chapter Notes

CHAPTER 2
What Matters Most?

Before we begin our time management journey, let's talk about what matters most to you. What's *really* important in your life today? Is it spending a lot of time with your family? Is it playing baseball as often as you can without throwing out your pitching arm? Is mastering that specific musical piece so you can one day become a classical pianist? Or is it just hanging out with your friends after a long day of school?

Whatever matters most to you will help you decide how to set your **goals**. Have you ever said, "I can do that!" after seeing someone play a sport or musical instrument? Right then and there, you decided that you would learn how to do it even if it took all week. That's called setting a **goal**.

Goal setting is something that each of us does without even realizing it, but it becomes very important as we choose how to spend our time. If we have no educational goals (for schoolwork), personal goals (for scouts) or sports goals (making the final cut for the basketball team), then we'll just go through

each day wondering what to do next. And we usually have a difficult time getting things done, because we don't know what to do first.

Let's take time to write down some goals that you would like to see happen in your life this year. Write down five of your biggest goals right here, and put a date beside them. Go ahead. I'll wait for you.

My Top Five (5) Goals:

1. _____

2. _____

3. _____

4. _____

5. _____

Next, write down *how* you can work toward those goals using action words, such as: **practice, learn, finish**, and so forth.

Do you need help getting started? No problem. Below is a sample of one of David's personal goals and how he plans to reach it.

All of David's goals are based on **action words** (remember learning about those in English class?). Action words, or verbs, convey action such as running, hopping or throwing. You can almost see something being done just from the word description, can't you?

An Action Plan for your goals will do the very same thing for you. It helps you to move closer to that goal that was so far away. Instead of saying, "I wish I knew how to play the guitar," David decided to take action. He made his top priority the goal of learning to play the guitar.

But instead of sitting back and waiting for the "guitar fairy" to visit him and make him an overnight expert, he took action and asked me to let him take lessons. And he made a point of taking action in the future (not just now at the beginning of setting his goal). His commitment to learn the parts of

---

My Top Five (5) Goals:

1. Learn how to play the guitar.

My Top Five (5) Goals Action Plan:

1. Learn the parts of the guitar.

2. Practice 30 minutes every day.

3. Play a song with the teacher in two weeks.

4. Play a song with Mom in one month.

My Top Five (5) Goals Action Plan:

1. _____

2. _____

3. _____

4. _____

5. _____

the guitar, play new chords, and then play a song with the teacher, are great ways to get started. He also set time-related goals when he decided to learn the song in two weeks and then play a duet with me in one month.

That's goal setting simplified and believe me, it really works! In fact, it works so well, that thousands of adults pay coaches and trainers a lot of money to teach them how to do it.

Now that you know the basics of goal setting, it's time to go back and finish listing your goals and the action steps that you'll take toward reaching them. Once you've finished, we'll learn more about the steps to becoming a time manager. We'll discover how to prioritize our tasks (or jobs) in the next chapter.

Chapter Notes

Dave SayZ ...

Choose what's more important to do and do it first so that you'll get it done sooner.

We can't all do everything...
~ Virgil

Chapter Notes

CHAPTER 3
Getting Your
Priorities Straight

Now let's discuss the Five Steps to Becoming a Successful Time Manager. I'll just introduce the steps for now, and then when we take a break, you can think of ways to customize this system for your own life. Instead of making a long list, make a point to **prioritize** your tasks so you can use goals to get things accomplished. **Delegate** effectively because you can't be in more than one place at once. **Limit your interruptions**, **consolidate** your tasks, and **use time blocks** for better organization.

Remember back in Section 1 when we made our Action Plan to clear the clutter? You chose the most cluttered area of your room and started right there—that was your highest priority for tackling the clutter in your house. Well, **prioritizing** simply means choosing what matters most to you and starting there first. Just as your dad uses the right tools for the right job when he's building something in his shop, you can use simple tools to prioritize your day, such as a **To-Do**

List. (A To-Do List is a list of jobs or tasks that you need to do in one day.)

If you're not a list maker, then just use your family's calendar. A wall calendar is easy to use and it's great way to see where you need to be and when you need to be there. In fact, most of us already have one posted in our homes somewhere.

If you already own a student planner or electronic PDA (personal digital assistant), then that's wonderful—please don't stop using what works best for you. But if you have found that what you've been using isn't working, don't feel like a failure and give up hope! This just means that you need to change your system to reflect your newly organized life. Believe me, this is totally normal.

Okay, here's a confession from a professional organizer: I've changed time management systems five times in the past seven years as my organizing needs have changed. Yep, that's right! Before I began my organizing company, I was a stay-at-home mom, and I bought a small notebook planner to store in my purse.

Then I switched to an organizing software when I spent most of my time online (reading emails and surfing the internet in my new home business). But when my son started preschool, and I got more involved with outside activities again, I switched to an electronic planner that I could toss into my purse and connect to my computer's software at home.

For a while, I was speaking and traveling away from home, so I switched to a small-sized notebook planner again. Then my son and husband (who are both huge electronics lovers) convinced me to at least *try* using a PDA.

They were right! Now I just love having access to that handy-dandy technology, and I wouldn't think of ever going back to using just a plain old planner again. Different activities call for different tools. (Gotta have the right tools for the right job, remember?)

? Did You Know?

PDA: a personal digital assistant is an electronic device that helps you with your time and your tasks.

Make it Personal

For those of you who are given a student planner during your first week of school, you probably realize how challenging it is to make someone else's system work for you. But after a week of struggling with *the system*, you might realize that it's not working for *you*. Well, managing your life as a student is the same as if you were trying to sit at your Dad's computer desk and use his new software. It's probably not too comfortable for you, and you wish you could adjust things a little bit.

Try to personalize your school's time management system by color-coding, adding on, or adjusting the system from time to time. You can still use it. Just customize it a bit to work better for your organizing style.

● **Color-coding** is great for those of us who remember best by seeing (visual learners). Write down assignments in different colors, using a different colored pen for each subject. For instance, Math assignments might be written in red, English in blue, and Social Studies in green. Or maybe you can use one color of ink for your schoolwork, and other colors for extra-curricular activities (such as red for Soccer, blue for piano lessons, and green ink for scouts.) These are just a few ways to make your planner more colorful so that it's more like you and less like someone else.

● **Adding on** is another way you can build onto the system that's already in place. Glue a copy of your daily schedule, chores, or notices inside your planner to help you remember the tasks that happen regularly. If you don't have a copy of your chore list, you can easily type one up on your computer using a word-processing program. Print it out as a portable reminder. I'm sure your mom or dad would be happy to help you create a chore list for your planner if you just asked them.

Another thing you can do to prioritize and manage your tasks is keep your daily To-Do List short and controllable. Some of you dear readers may struggle with ADD/ADHD, and the thought of more than five things on your list of To-Dos gives you a stomachache. That's okay. Keep your list short and move forward any of those things that didn't get done to the next day. You can also work from your Monthly Master List (like the Action Plan we learned about in Chapter 1) to make sure that you don't have unreasonable expectations each day.

Set Your Priorities

Try to rank or group your To-Dos by A, B, or C priority. (Please forgive me if this is a simple thing to understand, but not everyone has had time management training, so I like to start with the basics to make sure you are with me.)

● A-Priority

When making a **task list** (a list of things to do), you first need to choose the most important thing you *must* do today. Give it a ranking of **A or #1**. Color-code it on your schedule with a pen or stickers to make it easy to read.

I'm a visual learner, so I love things that are in color. I have found that other visual learners use all sorts of creative ways to emphasize important activities too, such as clipart, highlighters, or small stickers from an office supply store.

Make sure it's portable so you can grab it and go, then you won't have to take it off the fridge when you're leaving for a ballgame in a hurry. (Besides, Mom and Dad will need that calendar as well to keep up with the rest of your family activities!)

● B-Priority

Now do the same thing with your **B or #2** priorities. These are the things that don't necessarily have to be done first during the

45

day, but *should* get done sometime soon. An example of a B priority is working on that report that's due next week. If you can't get to it today, but you can go to the library tomorrow after school, then that will work, too.

• C-Priority

The **C or #3** priorities are usually the last thing on my list, and I'm lucky if I get them done during the week, much less every single day! So during your busy day, a C priority might be cleaning out your closet or learning how to play the guitar. Both are things that you really *could* do, but if you have other things that matter more, then these C priorities can wait for another day. Most of us bump these day after day until we finally have nothing else more important to do.

Now if some of these C priorities are jobs that you've been assigned by your parents (to clear out your closet by January 1st, let's say), then you'll have to do them eventually. Try tackling one C priority a day, and do a little at a time using **time blocks**. (We'll talk about time blocks later in this chapter.) Before you know it, those low priority jobs will finally be completed and you'll be a terrific time manager!

Now, finishing your homework is definitely an A priority, but organizing your closet or cleaning out your junk drawer, taking care of those things that are not

urgent, would be B and C priorities. It just depends who put them on your list. Helping Dad mow the yard comes first unless you have a history test tomorrow that you need to study for. (And if you've managed your time wisely, you won't have to cram for that test the night before anyway, right?)

? Did You Know?

priorities: sorting in order by putting the more important things first and the less important things last. **?**

If you are easily distracted, have ADD, or you're constantly interrupted, consider using note card system to help you manage your responsibilities. Neatly write one item on each card (the cards can be either 3x5 inches or 5x7 inches). Now group them according to tasks. Secure with a rubber band or store inside a box. If you really like things out in plain sight, mount a bulletin board on a wall or near your refrigerator (wherever you know it will be used).

Spread out the cards so that you can easily see what's on your To-Do List. As the items are finished, move them to the bottom of the row or pull them off entirely. How's that for a sense of accomplishment? Be sure to ask Mom or Dad for help with this project.

They may not want holes in the wall, and prefer that you prop up your bulletin board on the floor instead.

Keep it Portable

Your time management system doesn't have to be fancy, and you don't have to pay for expensive equipment either, but you should keep your system portable. Don't invest the money (and time) to create a new system and then let it gather dust in your backpack, desk, or drawer. Take the extra effort to make it work. Try to give this system three weeks before giving up on yourself.

Did you know that efficiency experts who study human behavior (yes, there really are people who do this type of thing for a living) have discovered that it takes an average of 21 days (that's three whole weeks) to create a habit?

So maybe you're quitting an old habit of not writing things down or always being late to class. In that case, it takes about three weeks to find out if this new time management system is really going to work for you. If not, then it's time to take another look, change whatever's not working, and then adjust it. Try not to give up on it completely. Stay on track!

Chapter Notes

_____

_____

_____

_____

_____

_____

_____

_____

_____

Chapter Notes

CHAPTER 4
Just Call for Help

The second characteristic of a successful time manager is being a **good delegator**. (Delegating means asking for help when you need it). As a young person, you probably are thinking, *who can I delegate to? I'm just a kid! I don't have a maid or robot to do everything I ask them to (and my little brother won't do it either!).*

But if there is one thing you can learn from this chapter, it's this: *you're not alone.* I'll bet when you first picked up this book to read, you felt like the most disorganized kid on the planet, right? You didn't have a clue about how to organize your closet or sort through the clutter in your family's garage. I know just how you feel, because each time I give a presentation at a conference, there is a room full of people—kids and grown-ups—just like you.

Now that should tell you something about being organized, shouldn't it? You're not alone, because others need to learn how to get organized too. And because some of us

are willing to share our challenges with others, you can learn how to find help for cluttered living.

Your Parents Are Just a Call Away

Did you know that your family is a just like a team that works together for the good of everyone, not just one or two people? When you *delegate* (there's that word again) chores, you're not only sharing responsibility to free yourself to do more kid things, but you are being an effective time manager too.

So if you're feeling overwhelmed with all the things you have to do today, don't be afraid to go to your parents and ask for their help. Tell them or show them what your list looks like. Ask for their advice in shuffling things around. They were a kid once too, you know. And they have some great ideas for making things easier on you and everyone else for that matter.

Look at your schedule together. Your parents may discover that you have too many activities after school, and suggest that you cut back to make time for what matters most to you. Maybe they can see that you have a full load of classes this year and need some more study time to keep those grades up. In fact, most parenting experts and teachers agree that students should not be involved in more than one outside activity during the school year. Don't be afraid to ask for help when you need it. Your parents are just a call away.

Also, if someone in your family asks for *your* help, be sure to help out when you can. Get the whole family involved in the planning stage, maybe through a family meeting. Put your heads together to decide what needs doing, when it should be done, and who needs to do it. Your mom usually has a Master List and will be happy to share this list with the rest of you! This really helps with the whole family's time management system. Since you are all working together on those chores, you'll have more free time, both

together as a family and separately with your friends.

 Dave SayZ ...

Use a chore chart for figuring out what you need to do for lessons and chores. This keeps your Mom or Dad from having to tell you what to do all the time.

Chore Charts Made Easy

Another delegating tool that has worked very well in our household is the Chore Chart. This works for the kids as well as grown-ups in our family. We can all see at a glance what needs to be done, and who needs to do it. If a chore is not getting done, we can all use our brains to figure out why. We can make changes in the system or take away a few privileges until the chores continue.

The man who does things makes many mistakes, but he never makes the biggest mistake of all — doing nothing.

~ Benjamin Franklin

Maybe your five-year-old brother Jon, who is in charge of taking out the trash, is too young to put out the trashcan each day, so Dad will need to do it instead. But Jon can certainly take over Dad's responsibility of feeding the cat each morning. Wow! Those chores are finally getting done. No one feels too overworked, and it was an easy solution to the problem, wasn't it? Writing down chores and dividing them up among family members really does simplify the job for everyone.

Some people think that Chore Charts are too much trouble or just for little kids. Positive encouragement through charting and rewards is one way to avoid family arguments. Instead of Mom getting mad at you when your chore isn't done, you'll be disappointed with yourself for not earning all your chore points this week and losing that reward. I'm sure that my family would much rather use a Chore Chart than to constantly hear me tell them to feed the dog, take out the trash, and brush their teeth!

🖐 Hands-On Time: The Family Chore Chart

Now it's time to take a break, grab a pad of paper, and have your mom and dad help you make a list of the household chores that need to be done around your house. Group them by how often they need to be finished: whether it's once a day, twice a week, once

a week, twice a month, once a month, every three months (quarterly), twice a year, or once a year (annually).

This isn't going to be permanent; it's just a starting point for your family's work schedule. Now review your list. Highlight or underline those chores that can be done less often and still keep up a level of cleanliness in your family's home. Boy, I wish I could give you a form here, but I'm afraid that I don't like housework, so my list is always changing. In fact, it's actually written in pencil so that I can adjust it often.

At one time, I used a laminated card that was stuck to the fridge with a magnet. Then I discovered that once I got into a routine, unplanned things happened. So I found myself starting back at square one. Remember to let this list of yours be a guide, and be ready with your handy-dandy eraser when things change in *your* family's household.

1. TELL your mom and dad that you need to have a business meeting with them. Schedule a good time for you to discuss the new game plan, let's say about 15 minutes. (Believe me, this is well worth the wait—who can even concentrate on creating a new family routine when the big game is on television or Dad's in the middle of balancing his checkbook?) Then sit down and review your list of chores *together*, adjusting it until it's a list that you all can live with.

2. SCHEDULE a family meeting to discuss the new Family Chore Chart. Arrange a time when each family member can be there to discuss the new changes in your household.

3. PRESENT your plan to the rest of the family, complete with a large version of the list on poster board or individual lists for each person to read. (You can type it and print it out using word-processing software on your computer.) Bring a Chore Chart to the meeting as a picture for everyone to see. Make this yourself or buy a simple chart from a teacher supply store—remember, it's the *process* that really works here, not the product. (That means it's the way you use it, not what you use).

4. ASSIGN chores to your family based on volunteers and assignments that are right for ages and abilities. For instance, a three-year-old can probably dust, feed the family pet, make her bed, and help empty the dishwasher. Elementary school children can empty trashcans, weed the garden, water the plants, and set the table for dinner. Middle schoolers can put out the trash, load recyclables into the van, mow the lawn, rake leaves, and vacuum. High school kids can help with laundry, clean out gutters, and take

younger children to and from school. I'm sure it won't take long before you have the basics for your new chore system.

5. LIST the chores and the name of the person who's responsible for doing them on the Chore Chart. Write it in pencil or use a wipe-off board—you'll probably be changing these quite a bit in the months to come.

6. DISCUSS the rewards and consequences of these chores with your parents. Whether your family uses stickers, checkmarks, or smiley faces on your chart is totally up to you. Be sure to use something that everyone likes to see every day to remind him or her to get his or her work done.

7. ESTABLISH a point system that is age appropriate and then keep it consistent. For instance, don't expect a toddler to do a lot of chores, or a preschooler to go all week before getting a reward—their little minds can't think that far ahead and by the time they get a treat for being good, they'll forget what it was for!

My son, David, at the time of this writing is nine. We've been charting his chores since he was three. Before that, we just told him what his chores were. He got a sticker for each task he completed throughout the day and a treat at the day's end. As he learned the system, and became a little bit more responsible, we eased him into a daily treat with only stickers for each task.

Then at age three-and-a-half we started the Chore Chart, using the same system we already had in place. He had three chores on his chart (which were blocked off Monday through Sunday, one square for each day), and they changed as he grew.

When we began using the chart, he was waking us up at 5:00 am each morning ready for the new day. His chart included: being quiet in the morning, feeding the cat, and putting away toys. We worked together on each task (he was, after all, only three!). Then he got instant feedback when the job was done. If he fussed about doing any of those chores, he got an X on his chart and didn't get his treat at the end of the day. Yikes! That was no fun at all.

When he reached a talking-back stage a few months later, we added a Bonus Chore: if he could go all day long without going into time out, he got a bonus regardless of the day's progress. If he was sick, we were traveling, or he just had a bad day, he could still earn some sort of **incentive** (reward). And it took out most of those temper tantrums, too!

At age five, he had four chores plus his bonus, which included: put away toys, stay quiet in the morning, feed the cat, and make

the bed. And he still had the bonus for no time-outs. Now at age nine, he has more chores since he is more responsible, such as: feed the dog, brush your teeth, wipe off the table, take out the trash, put away toys, and use good table manners. He also gets a bonus if he puts water in the birdbath without being asked, or picks up pinecones in the yard before his dad mows.

So here's the breakdown of the points system for our family: each time David does a chore, he gets to put a check mark on his chart. After dinner, if he has earned all his checkmarks, he gets a treat from the treasure box (which is a plastic box full of goodies such as sugar-free gum and candy).

Then I add points to his weekly total. He can earn up to three points a day, and as little as zero, depending on how he has completed his chores. When he has earned 20 points he gets to choose a special treat: a trip to the dollar store for a toy, a visit to the ice cream parlor, a bike ride with Dad, or something else that he values as a treat.

We started our weekly point system at five points, gradually moved it to seven, then twelve, fourteen, and now it's up to twenty. He may not earn all his points each week, but sometimes he has a great week and the points almost fly up on that chart! It all depends on his attitude and how badly he wants to earn it.

This type of system is called **positive reinforcement.** It's based on the discipline that's used in many schoolrooms across the country. I used positive reinforcement when I taught school many years ago, and now it's working in my own home, too. And the cool part is that it keeps us on a routine, we're less emotional, and we stay on task. It works so well for other families and I really think it will work for you and your family, too.

> *What lies behind us and what lies before us are tiny matters compared to what lies within us.*
>
> *~ Ralph Waldo Emerson*

Chapter Notes

_____

_____

_____

_____

_____

_____

_____

_____

_____

_____

_____

_____

Chapter Notes

Chapter Notes

CHAPTER 5
Hold the Phone

Being able to **limit interruptions** is the third quality of a successful time manager, which is a very important tool of time management. It works in an office for grown-ups, and I know that it will work for you at school and home, too.

Do you talk to your friends at school on Monday morning complaining about how tired you are and how busy your weekend was? Or do you cringe each time the phone rings just as you're finally concentrating on your math homework? Believe me, most of us do the very same thing without realizing how we are letting interruptions control us. But *you* are in control of your time, not your friends or classmates or even your sisters and brothers. In fact, you are the main person in control of your schedule and are responsible for setting the pace for yourself and your family, too.

I recommend that you start managing your time at home just as you would manage your time at school. Concentrate on the job that you're doing now, and block out all the other distractions. Start with simple time management tools such as these:

Don't Have An Open Door Policy

That means you shouldn't always answer the door or telephone if it means that it takes you away from something more important. Screen your phone calls and don't answer the door during restricted times. Stick to your rules, and share these rules with the rest of your family. Maybe the family rule is that nobody answers the door during dinnertime. Or you don't accept phone calls during homework time. Now this may sound a bit harsh, but if you're already having a tough time managing your time, then it's very important that you have a good plan and stick to it. Don't worry about what other people think—reclaim your time and get things done!

If you try this system for two or three weeks and it just doesn't work, then by all means change it a bit. Back off a little and limit the phone calls to a shorter period rather than not at all. Your friends will still be there after dinner and you can always call them back on the phone for a chat later. But you can't recapture family time when you discuss what's going on at school, in sports, and with your friends. (Not to mention the fact that you may need to ask Dad for an advance on your allowance or tell Mom that she needs to buy you a white shirt for your choir recital next week). Take advantage of closing the virtual door and don't have an open door policy in your organized home.

Use Power Tools

Let voicemail, caller ID or the answering machine be your personal secretary to screen your phone calls for you. Maybe you're hard at work finishing up a science fair project and the phone rings. Why not let the answering machine do its job by recording a message. You can return the call later when you're not so busy.

Learn to Say No!

Do you find yourself spending more time after school than you do at home? Or maybe you are always the first one the teacher calls on for extra-credit assignments, or the one your coach asks to make posters for the upcoming ballgame. Learn to say, "I need to think about it. Can I let you know later today?" That gives you a chance to look at your schedule, call your mom, or think about whether or not you're already overloaded for the day.

The same thing holds true for emails. Just because you receive an email or instant message (IM) doesn't mean that you need to drop whatever you're doing. You can respond later, especially if you're right in the middle of eating dinner, concentrating on a report, or helping your little sister with her homework. You really do need to focus on whatever you're doing at the moment. Try to filter out all those interruptions by using timesaving methods, not having an open-door policy, using power tools and just saying no. Who knows? Maybe you'll get so much homework done that you'll be able to play a little more of your favorite video game after dinner.

✋ Hands-On Time: Controlling Interruptions

Based on what you have just learned about limiting interruptions, complete the worksheet *Controlling Interruptions*. I've helped you by adding a couple of the most popular interruptions most kids have during the day, but I'm sure you'll have no trouble coming up with some of your own. Here's a hint: use the three timesaving methods that I listed earlier (no open door policy, using power tools, and saying no).

CONTROLLING INTERRUPTIONS WORKSHEET

Type of Interruption	Method of Control
doorbell rings during homework time	create a house rule for homework
phone rings during dinner hour	screen calls during dinner

Chapter Notes

Chapter Notes

Chapter Notes

CHAPTER 6
Time to Regroup

The fourth quality of a successful time manager is being able to **consolidate** tasks. Consolidating means grouping together. As you consolidate your errands and routine jobs, you'll discover time that you didn't even know you had. We all find ourselves saying, "I had no time this weekend. We spent all day Saturday running from soccer to baseball to my sister's gymnastics, and then we had to run errands with Mom, and then Sunday was church and then shopping at the mall, and…" (And we wonder why we get so cranky and drive our parents crazy! Hmm, wonder why?)

Time Blocks

I recommend that you limit your interruptions during the day (such as phone calls, emails and voicemails) so that you can focus on the task at hand. Then consolidate the rest and tackle them in either a single **time block** or a couple of smaller ones.

Time blocks are short segments of time, usually 10 or 15 minutes long, that you can use to get a job done. Sometimes just doing a little bit at a time helps tackle a big job, and keeps you from getting too tired as well. Believe me, it's much easier to work on cleaning out your closet or garage a few minutes at a time than to spend all day Saturday to get it done. This is an art. The more you practice it, the better you get at using time blocks to help manage your time wisely.

For example, you probably shouldn't take a phone call while writing a history report or solving math problems since the phone call interrupts your concentration. But when you've finished your A priority (the report), you can return all those missed calls at once (if you still have any energy left).

Let's say that it's your sister Lauren's turn to write down the phone messages that your family received during dinner. Your friends called, your dad's boss phoned…the list goes on and on. Ask Lauren to write them down so your family can organize and process them later. Are you going to return the calls after washing dishes or wait until tomorrow morning before school? If you are going to call them all back at once, whom do you call first? How do you prioritize all those callbacks?

Even though it's not your responsibility to return all those calls—just the ones that were for you—*someone* has to take down the messages and organize them. If you and your sister are willing to take turns, it will help your entire family to relax during dinner or during other busy times when they need to focus on their work. Maybe Lauren can write down the messages, then Mom can hand them out. Wow, you just delegated to Mom—how cool is that?

The process you use is your personal choice, but work-related messages for your parents are a higher priority than messages from your friends. Unless each person in your family has a cell phone of their own, you'll need to share the phone and take turns making callbacks. A call to a friend who's sad and needs some cheering up may need to be postponed until you can chat privately for a while. Maybe your family decides that it's first come, first served when it comes to messages.

In other words, the person who called earlier will be handled before the one who called later, and then it's on to #2, #3, and #4 in that order. Or you can prioritize what's most important to you. Your mom or dad is the best one to decide which system will work best for you and your family—I can't really give you a secret formula on this one.

Another task (or should I say tasks) to consolidate is errands. Most of us do this already without even realizing it, so I hope this is just a gentle reminder for you. Unless your mom or dad wants to get out on a daily basis, please try to limit your errand-running to one or two days a week rather than every day. Not only will you save gas (and money), you will also cut down on commute time as well.

We usually think of commuting as something a grown-up does when they go to or from work. But going to the dry cleaners during homework hours is based on the same idea. When you consolidate your tasks, remember that some commute time is wasted time and can be used more effectively, like working on your A and B priorities.

> *This time, like all times, is a very good one if we but know what to do with it.*
>
> ~ *Ralph Waldo Emerson*

Special NeedZ ...

Wear a digital watch with an alarm. Set it to remind you to check blood sugar levels, take medication, or go to a doctor's appointment.

Dave SayZ ...

Have your Mom or Dad give you a "5-Minute Warning" before you need to finish what you're doing. This helps you quickly get your work done without feeling all stressed out.

Chapter Notes

_____

_____

_____

_____

_____

_____

_____

_____

_____

_____

_____

_____

Chapter Notes

CHAPTER 7
Building Blocks of Time

The fifth feature of a good time manager is being able to use **time blocks** wisely. Remember earlier when I discussed how to take 10 or 15 minutes at a time to chip away at that big project of yours? Now it's time to take your #1 or A Priority tasks and finish those first.

If you want to do them all at once then go ahead and use one big time block to take away the stress. Or allow 10-15 minutes for a B Priority. This will change with your To-Do List from day to day. Believe me, those 15 minutes really do add up over time! (We'll talk more about this later in the 15-Minute Challenge™ at the end of the book.)

For example, if you have several errands to run all over town with Dad, obviously you will need to save some of your To-Dos for tomorrow (or the next errand day in their schedule). That's okay. You don't have to finish each and every thing on your To-Do List. Wow, did you read that correctly? You sure did! I hereby give you permission *not* to complete your To-Do List *every* day. Woo hoo! What a relief.

That means that you don't have to stay up until 10:00 pm at night organizing your closet or cleaning out the garage. And your family certainly doesn't need to run 10 errands in a single day, draining the car and the energy of everyone in it!

In fact, one of my organizing clients told me she was so frustrated with her family's schedule that just being able to cross *one* thing off her To-Do List each day was a major milestone. She had set her standards so high that she didn't know where to start (or where to stop, either). But now her family is able to group their errands together, spending more time at home and less time on the road. Now that's what I call being a great time manager!

Chapter Notes

CHAPTER 8
Time-Wasters
and Time-Savers

I'd like to share some bonus tips with you that I call **time-wasters**. They fall under the category of interruptions, errands, chores, and time management. First, I'll state a problem, and then present a solution for each one. This information is to help you think about what you've learned so far about time management and the creative ways that you can control your own schedule during the day. Ready? Okay, let's get started.

Time-Waster: Interruptions

Let's say that the biggest time-waster of the day at your house is interruptions, such as the doorbell and telephone. Unless you live in a cave, you will have many interruptions. There's just no getting around it! What do you do?

Time-Saver: Establish an Interruption Policy

Have an interruption policy where your family screens visitors and phone calls to avoid those interruptions. Enforce the family rules such as no calls during dinner, no calls after 8:00 pm, or no calls during study time.

Remain in control of the chaos creators in your family's life. These are just examples, but I'm sure your mom and dad can come up with some great tips on their own. And of course, you should discuss any rules with your parents before starting to use them.

Time-Waster: Errands

Running errands with Mom or Dad seems to be a never-ending part of your life. It sure seems like such a waste of time, doesn't it? Is there a solution?

Time-Saver: Consolidate

When you need to run errands, try to consolidate them (as you learned earlier). Also, plan your route before you leave. Just as you plan a route on the map before going on vacation, you can plan your course for Errandland, too. Or if you're going to a place that you've never been before, just make a copy of your city's map, and use a highlighter to trace your route on the copy. Now Mom can glance at it as she's driving down the busy freeway. This is a great time-saver when you live in the city and you need to

69

pick up a band uniform from the new store across town, plus have your instrument tuned at the music store, and then tag along to your little brother's piano lesson. Whew!

If you're just running errands close to home, try to avoid running back and forth. I actually know people who go to the dry cleaners, return home to pick up videos only to double back to the video store right next door to the cleaners! Try to help your mom (or dad) to create a route where you're not crisscrossing over your path too many times.

Keep a tote bag or a plastic crate in your closet or near the front door for outgoing things. Just grab your tote, and head right out the door for a quick trip to Errandland without having to run back inside to grab a book or video.

Time-Waster: Chores

Chores are a huge time-waster, so I really would like to encourage you to get help with these. Look back at our chapter about Chore Charts so that you can make the most of delegating. But to review, let's find a simple solution.

Time-Saver: Chore Chart

Call a family meeting to establish who does what and when. When you discuss all the chores that you are responsible for, your family will be able to help you create your To-Do List. This is a good example of talking

things out instead of trying to guess what everyone needs. And don't forget to keep in touch with your parents about what's gobbling up your time. Don't be afraid to ask for help when you need it.

You know, this is actually something a good manager does on a regular basis at work. Unless one day you become the owner of a company, you will report to somebody at some level. When you become frustrated and ask your boss for help, you'll be practicing good time management skills. You may find yourself saying, "I'm sorry but I can't do all this. You gave me 12 things to do today and I only have time for five. I really need help!" At some point, you will have to decide whether to fall apart or ask for help. A good manager will then take a look at your task list of things to do and say, "Okay, let's give these three things to Ernie, these four things to Paula, these four things to you, and I'll do this one." Now that's a great way to divide and conquer!

Did you know that you could easily do the same thing as a time manager? Just politely give it over to your parents so they can figure out what needs doing, what can wait, and just how well it needs to be done. There's no rush to do everything all at once if you can just use little time blocks here and there. When your family thinks it's time to get something done, turn off the TV, grab the vacuum cleaner, and perform a little damage control. Remember, you're all a team and teamwork is much better than working alone. And if you really want to have a great reminder, think of the word TEAM. There is no letter "I" in that word. Keep working together and you really can make a difference.

Try to manage your schedule by using a Chore Chart or a planner. Write it down, keep it in your backpack, or post it on the fridge. As the needs in your family change, take the time to have family meetings so your parents can shuffle things around to adjust the responsibilities. I hope that you'll learn to delegate as much as you can and get help from your family team members when you most need it. After all, that's what they're there for.

✋ Hands-On Time: No Time to Waste

Complete the worksheet, **How Do You Waste Your Time?** First, read the list of time-wasters in the left-hand column. Then rank them in number order from 1-5, with #1 being the biggest waster and #5 being the smallest waste of time. Be honest while doing this exercise—take the time to do some heavy-duty thinking to see how you *really* spend your time. I think the answers may surprise you!

Based on the time management techniques you've learned in this chapter,

How Do You Waste Your Time?	
Time-waster	**Ranking**
Not asking for help	_____
Dealing with clutter	_____
Putting things off	_____
Deciding what to do first	_____
Interruptions	_____

make an effort to change at least *two* of the items on your list this month. Feel free to write notes to yourself (as a reminder) using the **Two-week Progress Report** on the next page. Change your priorities and get rid of those distractions!

Look back at your worksheet again in *two weeks* to check your progress. Follow-up again in *one month*. Be sure to mark it on your calendar and then make a date for success. Did you reach your goal? If so, congratulations! You're now ready to tackle two more time-wasters next month. Oh my, did you veer off course? That's okay. You just need to slow down and focus on getting rid of at least one of the time-wasters in your life next month. Keep working on it. You can do it!

Two-week Progress Report

#1 Time-waster to change   **Deadline**   **Date Changed**

_____

_____

#2 Time-waster to change   **Deadline**   **Date Changed**

_____

_____

Chapter Notes

_____

_____

_____

_____

_____

_____

_____

_____

_____

_____

_____

Chapter Notes

Chapter Notes

CHAPTER 9
Time to Go

All of us are bombarded with stuff all day long. From school assignments to after-school activities, it's no wonder we forget things more than we remember them. But that's actually quite normal. Even the most organized people use lists and prioritize their tasks as a way to keep on schedule and eliminate brain clutter, even the experts.

Take the time to write down school assignments and keep them in one place. If you don't like using a planner, then choose a colorful spiral notebook, binder, or legal pad. Any tool will work as long as you keep all your notes in one place. Be sure to carry this to class with you so you can capture those notes. Bring it home each day in your book bag – now there's no pressure to rely on your memory any more! Writing it down is the easy part of time management. Now let's learn how to follow through.

Consistency is Key. Sounds like a television ad, doesn't it? But it's so true. You need to create a time management routine where you check your Master List of To-Do's

every single day. Talk with your parents about your schedule and then ask them to help you figure out when it's the best time to review your agenda each day. Ask Mom or Dad to help you think ahead, using a monthly calendar, planner, or other cool scheduling tool. You know, most kids really can't even remember what they ate for breakfast or think about what they'll be doing tomorrow night. They just live for the moment. Not having to worry about things is the best part of being a kid! And with your parent's help, you too can learn to set monthly goals, create a weekly schedule, and plan your day one step at a time.

Now that you've learned all the steps to discovering more hours in your day and how to manage your time, let's talk about those pesky papers that seem to multiply in your desk, shall we? And what's up with all that stuff that comes home in your backpack and finds its way into your closet? Let's learn how you can set up a file system that works for you and helps you manage the papers that follow you home.

Chapter Notes

SECTION 3

Follow That Paper Trail

CHAPTER 1
Paper Management
Made Easy

Paper clutter is such a challenge. It can quickly take over our homes, filling every box and drawer until they overflow. But you really don't need to let paper piles take over your room or backpack. In fact, with a simple plan, you can set up and manage your organizing system to keep the paper clutter under control.

Before we get started down that paper trail, I've got to make another confession: I don't like paperwork! Nope, not at all. In fact, filing is my least favorite thing to do. I'd much rather delegate this to someone else in our family. But then how would I find information on David's MP3 player when it needs to go to the shop for maintenance? Or how would I know that our subscription for Highlights for Children® magazine is about to end? Maybe filing isn't such a waste of time after all.

Actually, managing paper clutter is just like managing all the other areas of our lives. We need to *file as we go* to keep it under control—just as we clean as we go to keep

our room clutter from overwhelming us. Otherwise we'd be like one of my clients who didn't file her paid bills (or anything else) for over a year. Yikes! What a mess her desk was! It took us awhile to figure out the best system for her to use. However, after just two weeks of sorting through the stacks a little bit each day, she was finally able to see the top of her desk again. Now, seven years later, she's still filing as she goes and putting paper in its proper place. That's a great success story, isn't it?

> *The trail is the thing, not the end of the trail. Travel too fast and you miss all you are traveling for.*
>
> *~ Louis L'amour*

Looking back through the books and articles that I've written over the years, I'm noticing that there just aren't a lot of tips that I've written about paper management. There's a definite pattern here. Not that I don't think it's important, but it's just not something that I'm all that excited about. On the other hand, I *really* get excited about de-cluttering closets, creating chore charts, using a PDA, and organizing your car. But I personally don't enjoy filing and so that's not something I specialize in as a personal organizer. However, talking with moms, dads, and kids over the years has shown me that this *is* something that *is* important to them. In fact, sometimes the paper clutter threatens to take over their homes, offices, and backpacks. Yikes!

So I guess to manage this paper problem, we need to start at the very beginning—learning about the different types of filing systems and how to create them. We'll also study how to maintain clutter so that papers don't leave a trail across your kitchen, down the hall and into your bedroom where they settle into a huge stack that refuses to leave. We'll learn about the two types of files, **current** and **archive**, and how to treat them differently. Are you ready to tackle those stacks yet? Good, then let's get started.

Special NeedZ ...

Write down everything you need to remember in a journal or spiral notebook. Keep it near your medical equipment. For example, a diabetic might need food intake or insulin charts. Someone with food allergies might need to keep a record of everything he eats between testing for reactions. Now there's no need to rely on your elusive memory when you're visiting with the busy doctor!

Be of good cheer. Do not think of today's failures, but of the success that may come tomorrow. You have set yourselves a difficult task, but you will succeed if you persevere; and you will find joy in overcoming obstacles. Remember, no effort that we make to attain something beautiful is ever lost.

~ Helen Keller

Chapter Notes

Chapter Notes

CHAPTER 2
Awesome
Paper Organizing

Let's start by using the four steps of awesome organizing. Remember you learned about these steps when you set up your own clutter management system? We'll go through the steps together: plan, sort, organize, and maintain.

1. Plan for Success

Write down some notes to determine what kinds of papers you have, where you think they should be stored, what you'll need for storage, and how you will keep it going once it's created. Then you can start sorting! (If you need a refresher course for sorting, you can turn to Section 1, or just sit tight until we get to the Hands-On Time that's coming up next.)

2. Sort through your Stuff

This is the fun part, which you can do effortlessly in front of the television or while listening to your favorite music. Grab a few sturdy boxes (or the ones you used from

before in your other organizing project), and then begin going through the paper piles one at a time. Sort papers, magazines, and catalogs into categories, grouping like things together. Keep sorting until you're finished!

Of course, you can always tackle this in bite-sized time blocks if that works better for you. Sometimes we just don't have enough time to sit down for several hours to get a job done. That's when time blocks come in handy. Just set a timer for 15 minutes, and sort as much paper as you can until it goes off. Shove your stacks aside for later or process those papers as you go—it's really up to you whatever method you choose to help you get through this step in the organizing process.

🖐 Hands-On Time: Do the Paper Shuffle

Use three of the labels from your previous organizing projects (KEEP, TRASH,

UNDECIDED) or create new ones as you set up sorting boxes for this part of your Hands-On Time activity.

Stick your signs to the boxes with tape so that you can use them over again. (Unless you're super organized, you'll end up organizing papers and other clutter another time. You might as well save time and energy by recycling your labels, right?)

Try to make a point not to read every single piece of paper that you pick up, otherwise this stage of organizing can really come to a standstill. If you're sorting a new stack of papers, you might want to add a fourth sorting box—TAKE ACTION—but be sure to label it. This will hold those papers that call for action on your part, such as: permission slips that need signing for a field trip, reading assignments to post in your planner, or a report that needs to be filed in your file system. We'll get to that file system later on in this section.

Since you're just sorting and categorizing by *type* (magazines, notes, reports, completed homework, tests, and so forth) or *action* (needs signing, needs paying, post in planner, or file in binder), it's *easy* to breeze through this stage once you get into the

> *Out of clutter, find simplicity*
> *~Albert Einstein*

Did You Know?

File System: folders with tabs that are categorized to organize your important papers.

rhythm of sorting. Be sure to have those large sturdy boxes near you. That way you won't have to worry about paper overflow onto the floor or slumping garbage bags.

3. Organize What's Left

Now that you've gone through your papers, it's time to organize them so that you don't have to keep repeating this dreadful step each month (or week, in some cases). We're going to create two different sets of files, current files and archived files.

PAPER WORK

Use the "Paper Work" form (shown on the next page) to plan your attack on the paper monster in your home. List the types of papers that will be stored in your **current files** and **archive files.** If you trust your memory, leave out the writing step and move on. You can skip over the writing part if you're not much of a "write-things-down" sort of person, but please don't skip the actual planning. This stage allows you to stop

PAPER WORK FORM:

<u>CURRENT FILES</u>

History report

Field Trip form

Last week's spelling test

Progress report

_____

_____

_____

_____

_____

_____

_____

_____

_____

_____

_____

_____

_____

<u>ARCHIVE FILES</u>

Last week's homework

Guitar lesson receipts

Math semester test

4-H Ribbons

_____

_____

_____

_____

_____

_____

_____

_____

_____

_____

_____

_____

_____

and evaluate where your paperwork will actually be stored.

CURRENTLY IN USE

Current files are made up of things that you use daily or weekly, such as: fees to be paid, appointments to be made, and anything else requiring action (either today or in the near future). These current files might include an appointment reminder from your dentist, a band camp sign-up form, or a progress report from your homeroom teacher.

Create simple categories for these things with names that make sense to you. Keep the stacks separated in manila folders or stacking bins. (I really like folders better than bins or trays because you can store them vertically (up and down instead of stacked in piles across your desk or table. Stacking bins are just one more place to gather clutter!).

Dave SayZ ...

Put paper into a filing system so you know where all your papers are, and they're organized.

Color-code your current files if you think it will help you stay focused. Use either colored folders or colored dots placed on plain folders. Store papers in a vertical stair-step rack on your desk or countertop, or in a small crate or your desk drawer. Just don't file these away so safely that you forget where they are and stop using them altogether!

IT'S ALL IN THE SYSTEM

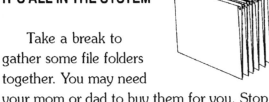

Take a break to gather some file folders together. You may need your mom or dad to buy them for you. Stop your organizing process for now until you can get these ready. You'll need the following supplies to set up your kid files system:

• **Hanging Folders** – You can use either letter or legal sized folders, depending on your file holder. Buy either plain green or colorful folders, whatever is within your paper-organizing budget. You did make a budget, didn't you? If not, this is a good time to go back to the planning stage of your paper organizing so that you can decide how much money you actually have to spend on organizing your papers. For special storage needs, try to locate folders with a special pocket for CDs or diskettes.

• **Folder Tabs** – I suggest you use clear plastic tabs so you can read your labels easily. Although colored tags are pretty, it's not much fun trying to read your labels through them. This can slow you down when you file or try to find something fast. These tabs usually come in the box with your hanging folders, so you probably won't have to buy extra ones.

• **Manila Folders** – Manila folders are file folders that your teacher or parents use in their file cabinet to hold important papers. They are usually a creamy beige color. Although they're not too exciting to look at, they do a good job of containing important papers. File folders are sold in two different types: 5-cut or 3-cut. As you hold a folder in front of you, look at the tab or notched portion at the top—that's the "cut". In a box of folders, there are folders that are grouped by 3's or 5's, depending on the width (or size) of the notch. A 3-cut folder will have wider tabs so that you can write long words on them. A 5-cut folder will have a narrower tab instead.

The main reason that the tabs are different widths is to allow for folders to be filed without a hanging folder inside a file cabinet. If you placed several file folders in a file cabinet (or box), one behind the other, it would be hard to read the label written on the tab unless they were staggered or moved over a bit. So the folks who make the folders came up with a system years ago to help you. That's where the idea of 3-cut or 5-cut folders came from.

For some reason, most offices use 5-cut folders, but we professional organizers like to use 3-cut because they're much easier to read and use. And we all know that if you can't read it, you won't use it, right?

• **Label Markers** – Many people put off using file folders because they think fancy labels need to be created with a label maker or computer. But that's just not so! All you need to make your files work for you are a steady hand and a felt-tip marker. But of course, if you already have a handy-dandy label maker, then this is a great time to use it. It will definitely make your organizing time more fun.

I recommend black or dark blue ink for your pen so you can read your labels easily; otherwise you'll spend time writing down what's inside the folder and won't be able to read it later. That would be a poor waste of time, indeed.

• **Folder Labels** – Folder labels are optional for your filing system. Not only are they expensive, but also it's hard to stick them onto the folder tabs straight. This is a filing supply that's definitely an option. You don't have to use it if you don't want to.

After you gather your filing supplies together, put them off to one side until you finish planning and sorting through your papers. You will use them later to organize your paperwork.

INTO THE ARCHIVES

Now that we've discussed what to do with your current files, let's take a look at another type of file you'll be working with. **Archived Files** are those you've already done something with but need to keep such as: receipts for membership or lessons, warranties for your Game Boy® and such. These are files that you don't use on a regular basis but need to keep for a while.

They should be stored in your file crate or in a sturdy box. Put them in a file folder and then place the manila folder inside a hanging folder. Be sure to clean these out (sort and toss) once a year to make room for new archived files.

 **Dave SayZ ...**

Make a TO READ folder so you know where to go when you want to read magazine articles. Tear out the article and then toss the rest of the magazine in the trash.

Make a point to label your boxes before storing them so you can find papers in a hurry when your MP3 player needs fixing or you want to look back on old reports from last year.

Sort your paperwork as it arrives in your home—right after you bring it home from school, sports, or you open your mail. Divide papers into categories such as To File, To Toss, To Pay, To Call, Follow Up Later, and so on. Those become the titles or labels on your file folders, and make this whole process much easier to work with. Store your papers together in manila folders, pocketed folders, a binder with pocketed dividers, or an accordion file. The tool doesn't matter, but your system *does*.

Feel free to keep using a system that you've already created. Adjust it with color, labels, and the current/archive method to make it work for your organizing style. And remember to sort through and toss out once a year so that your files don't get too full.

✋ Hands-On Time: Just File It

Complete the worksheet **Where Would You File This?** found on the next page. Based on the four steps of organizing and the paper management skills you've just learned, decide where you would put each piece of paper listed on the form. For example, the third paper item on the list, Arts & Craft Article, might be filed in a folder labeled "To Read" until you can find time read the entire article. You may want to file it in your arts & crafts folder instead.

Depending on its priority, assign a home for paperwork until you can take action. Have you noticed that there isn't a right or wrong answer here? We all think differently, organizing in our own unique way. Just put it where you will go to look for it—it's that easy!

4. Maintain Your System Every Day

As for those articles you might read later, and the rest of the daily paper clutter that you've saved, try to clip and toss as much as possible. When you bring papers home from school, clip articles and file them later in a notebook or photo album. Toss the remainder of the magazine to avoid clutter overload on your bookcase or magazine rack.

This is something you don't want to do if you share a subscription with your brother or your parents! But if the magazine is all yours and you've finished reading it, keep the parts that you need. Store the article in a folder labeled "To Be Read" until you have the time to read it. Place it in your archive files if you think that you'll need it later for a report or term paper.

Once you start practicing this type of clutter control, you'll find much more space on your bookcase, too.

Once you've sorted through the paper clutter, gathered organizing materials together, and set up your system, you'll be using it every day to control paper clutter at school and home.

Make a habit of emptying your backpack when you get home from school. Sort and process the papers instead of tossing them onto the kitchen table or giving them to your mom.

At the end of each nine weeks, reorganize your files. Pull out unused papers to toss, and move important papers to archive boxes to save. Then once a year, box up your archived papers and treasures, write the year on the outside, and move it out of the main area of your filing system. This creates a home for next year's papers and frees up valuable space in your workspace, too.

WHERE WOULD YOU FILE THIS?

TYPE OF PAPER	FILE NAME
Permission slip	Current File: Needs Action
Last year's report card	Archived File: By Year
Arts & crafts article	_____
Old reports	_____
Graded homework	_____
4-H ribbons	_____
Note from a friend	_____
Photographs	_____
_____	_____
_____	_____
_____	_____
_____	_____
_____	_____
_____	_____

PORTFOLIOS ARE FUN

We've talked about organizing your papers into files, but what about those papers that are part of your studies and will be part of your student record?

Although you're not quite ready to go to college yet, one day you might want to get a degree and have a professional job. Whenever high school students prepare for college, they have a short interview with someone on the staff at the college they'd like to attend. Sometimes it's a short meeting, and other times it's a formal interview with several people at the college of your choice. They will look at their student file (hopefully they keep well organized files, too) that contains your test scores, personal information, and activities that you've been involved in.

But what if you're one of many students who qualify for their college and they can only accept a few this year? How do you think they decide who will join their course of study? That's when a student portfolio comes in handy.

A **portfolio** is a special file that you or your parents keep throughout your studies. It will show your special interests, projects, and volunteer activities. Boy scouts, 4-H and volunteering at a hospital or nursing home are all wonderful reflections of who you are and how you lead others. Sometimes parents start a portfolio for their children when they are young, and then encourage their kids to add to it over the years. Other parents aren't so organized and scramble to gather papers and certificates together right before high school graduation. But with a few tips to get you started, this is a project that you can do mostly by yourself as you go.

Remember earlier in this chapter when we learned about sorting through our papers? I suggested that you make stacks of your papers for things that needed to be read, paid, or filed away. And when it was time to file, you learned how to file in either current files (that you use almost everyday) or archive files (papers that need to be kept for later use). Some archived files are never used again, and can be tossed after a year or so (such as a subscription to your favorite magazine). But other archived files need to be looked at months or even years later.

Building your portfolio is important business if you want to become an artist, musician, researcher, or other trained professional. Let's take a look at some of the ways we can build a portfolio and examples of each.

• **Tag, You're It!** – Tag board (or poster board) makes a wonderful material for a simple portfolio. Take two pieces of poster board, place one on top of the other, and tape them together on three sides with masking tape. You should now have an open pocket to fill with artwork, poetry, certificates, or awards. Store it flat under the bed or standing upright between your desk and the wall.

• **Out of the Box** – Clean pizza boxes found at an art supply store can hold all kinds of important papers for your portfolio. Larger than a regular storage box but small enough to stack in your closet, these boxes will keep your designs dry and your awards contained. Just toss in 4-H ribbons, photos of your science project, and your award-winning essays to keep safe until you need them. Do not—I repeat, do not—reuse pizza boxes to store your papers. Your important things might smell like pepperoni for years to come, and it would be a great shame to ruin them!

• **In a Bind** – Three-ring binders or notebooks are probably the most common type of portfolio. They're  easy to use, too. Almost anyone can take a binder, fill it with plastic pockets, and create a simple collection of their activities. Have you seen clear sheet protectors that Mom uses for scrapbooking or Dad uses to store his computer booklets?

Those clear pockets are the best tools for safekeeping your valuable certificates, examples of your writing, and photographs of you with your prize-winning invention.

Whatever method you choose to store your school keepsakes, be sure to label them with a descriptive title (what it is) and the date (month and year). If you can't keep every piece of paper or a huge project board from the science fair, take good photos and display them in your portfolio instead. You will do so many wonderful things in your life.

A portfolio is a great way to organize them. You thought you were just organizing as you go just to be an awesome organizer, but you're really organizing for the future. How cool is *that*!

 **Dave SayZ ...**

Keep a separate pile for your artwork and special papers. Put these into a box or folder to save.

Chapter Notes

Chapter Notes

Chapter Notes

Chapter Notes

CHAPTER 3
Thanks for the Memories

Hidden Treasures

Well, it's finally time to talk with you packrats out there. I think you know who you are. You save every gum wrapper, card, and newspaper clipping that you've ever had. Maybe for a while you've been able to stash them in a shoebox, but those are quickly filling up and overflowing, too. Or perhaps you've just left them on the top of your desk or in a box on the closet floor. Whatever do you do with all that stuff?

Let's tackle these stacks as we would any other stacks of clutter. Learning from our lessons in paper management earlier in this chapter. Make a plan for where you're going to store them (a treasure zone). Sort through the stacks and place them in categories. Next, organize them into a container.

As you sort through your treasures, you'll probably see different types of things like: ribbons, trophies, notes, birthday cards, project boards, models, and lots of pictures. Just start sorting, and remember the most

important rule of organizing is do not get too attached! Don't stop to read every note and card. Go through the box, keeping only the things that are dear to you. Toss out things that aren't, and put aside those things that you're not sure about. If you feel you can't get rid of a single thing, then it's time to call in a clutter buddy.

Grab your best friend, your mom, or someone else who can help you decide what to keep and what to toss. Let them be the one to pick up each thing so you don't get too sad over letting it go. Some examples of things to keep might be:

- pictures of you at the science fair with your project board
- a certificate from space camp
- a drawing that won first prize at the art fair

You can probably toss most of the birthday cards you saved for the past ten years, unless you want to keep one from someone special to remember him or her by. And if you're not sure about something, like a trophy or project board, ask your Mom or Dad about storage space in the basement or attic. If there isn't room for storing these bulky treasures, take a picture of them as a replacement for the trophy.

Once you've worked through your entire collection, you can finally begin organizing. Use the same tools for organizing treasures as you did for organizing your clutter in Section 1. Plastic tubs, under-the-bed boxes, and sturdy containers make solid treasure zones for your special things. You'll add to your treasure box in the years to come, so

store them in a larger container than you currently need. That will leave room for your collection to grow without smashing important papers or crunching blue ribbons.

If you want to be a little more creative, talk with your parents about ways to create a scrapbook for your treasures. Maybe you want to even start a photo album of your own with those pictures left over from your sorting project. Perhaps you can share them with friends and family. Whether you have one box or several, taking the time to properly label and store your treasures will keep them safe for years to come.

Chapter Notes

_____

_____

_____

_____

_____

_____

_____

_____

SECTION 4

Closing Thoughts

Closing Thoughts

Congratulations! You've graduated from the ranks of the cluttered and have become another one of those Organized Kidz™. Whether you're trying to organize stuff in your bedroom, bathroom, or car, now you can use ideas you've learned in this book to organize any area of your life. Just remember the Four Steps for Awesome Organizing (plan, sort, organize and maintain), the Five Steps to Becoming a Successful Time Manager (limit interruptions, delegate, use time blocks, set priorities, and consolidate your tasks), and how to tame the paper trail.

Now, go out and conquer that clutter! It's time to make order out of chaos; to spend less time cleaning and more time hanging out with your friends and family. Get ready to manage your time wisely and create more hours in your day for fun.

So, are you finally ready for the 15-Minute Challenge™ I told you about earlier in our organizing journey? Good, I thought so! Your challenge (should you choose to accept it) is to take 15 minutes a day to clear the clutter on your desk, in your room, or in the shared living spaces of your house. Make sure you take the time every day to maintain the new organizing system for your closet, files, and schedule. Make an appointment with yourself in your planner until it becomes automatic. Set a timer to race your brother as you pick up household clutter or beat your own personal time for collected stuff. You can do it! You've worked so hard to earn the title of an Awesome Organizer and to live a wonderfully organized, balanced life. Happy organizing, and God bless!

Alone we can do so little;
together we can do so much.
~ Helen Keller

About the Authors

Debbie Williams is a professional organizing strategist, parent educator and author. She is the founder of *Organize Your Home Day*™ and editor of the online organizing site, **OrganizedTimes.com**.

David Williams is a homeschooled student with an *eye* for detail. An inventor since the age of four, David plans to attend university upon graduation so he can pursue a career in physical science or engineering. Currently he enjoys math, science, photography, playing guitar, and hanging out with his dog, Caeleigh.

How to Contact the Authors

We'd love to hear from you. Feel free to share your success stories with us, as well as the challenges of your organizing experience. Let us know what works for you and your family, as well as the creative ways that you have modified the organizing systems to make them your own.

You can write to us at:
**Debbie Williams or David Williams
c/o By the Book Media
P.O. Box 590860
Houston, TX 77259**

Or send us an email:
info@organizedtimes.com

We'll be happy to post your stories and before and after pictures on our Organized Kidz™ website. Your stories will encourage other kids to become Awesome Organizers, too. Pass it on!

And if Mom or Dad needs some help getting organized, they can visit our website at: www.OrganizedTimes.com to find more tools to help their family team in the organizing journey.

APPENDIX

Useful Tools for Organized Kids and Their Families

1. Getting the Right Tools
2. Alternative Organizing Solutions (Answer Key)

Getting the Right Tools

Storage Solutions

Box4Blox™ Block Organizers
www.box4blox.com

Custom and Semi-Custom Closet Organizers
California Closets
www.californiaclosets.com

Shelves, Bins and Racks
Ikea
www.ikea-usa.com

Days of the Week Closet Organizers
Lillian Vernon Corporation
www.lillianvernon.com

Folders and Pockets for Paper Organizing
Mead
www.mead.com

Rolling Carts with Drawers
Office Max
www.officemax.com

Clearview Case Binders™ from UniKeep
www.unikeep.com

Time Savers

Daily Planners
At-a-Glance®
www.at-a-glance.com

Daily Planners
Daytimer®
www.daytimer.com

Visual Pocket Organizer
EZ Pocket®
www.ezpocket.com

School Agendas
FranklinCovey
www.franklincovey.com

Planning Boards & Schedulers
The Planning Centre
www.marshplan.com

Digital Watch with Timer
Watchminder®
www.watchminder.com

Thinkbin™
Thinkbin Family Calendar
www.thinkbin.com

Helpful Websites

ADHD of the Christian Kind
www.christianadhd.com

Family Life
www.familylife.com

Focus on the Family
www.focusonthefamily.org

Crown Financial Ministries
www.crown.org

Organized Times
www.organizedtimes.com

Books for Parents

All About Talent: Discovering Your Gifts and Personality by Larry Burkett, Cook Communications, ISBN 0781437873

Common Sense Organizing: A Step-by-Step Program for Taking Control of Your Home and Your Life by Debbie Williams, Champion Press Ltd, ISBN 1932783261

Creative Correction by Lisa Whelchel, Tyndale House Pub., ISBN 1561799017

Grace-Based Parenting by Tim Kimmel, W Publishing Group, ISBN 0849905486

Life Skills for Kids: Equipping Your Child for the Real World by Christine Field, Shaw Pub., ISBN 0877884722

Mom Central by Stacy deBroff, Kodansha America, ISBN 1568362196

Money Doesn't Grow on Trees: Teaching Your Kids the Value of a Buck by Ellie Kay, Revell, ISBN 0800787250

Personality Plus for Parents by Florence Littauer, Baker Book House Co., ISBN 800757378.

The Blessing, by John Trent and Gary Smalley, Nelson Books, ISBN 0785260846

The Five Love Languages of Children by Gary D Chapman and Ross Campbell, Moody Publishers, ISBN 1881273652

The Way They Learn by Cynthia Tobias, Focus on the Family Pub., ISBN 1561794147

Alternative Organizing Solutions (Answer Key)

Wooden Cigar Box – Makes a decorative holder for all those remote controls, a message center near the phone, or an arts and crafts box.

Film Canister – Store spare change, lunch money, vitamins, paper clips and thumbtacks in your desk drawer.

Makeup Bag – Serves as a portable school supply drawer for backpack or locker, a comb and mirror for the car, or first aid kit for your beach bag.

Zippered Pencil Case – Holds art supplies for the backseat of the car, contains pens and pencils in the junk drawer of your desk, is a desk drawer for your backpack.

3-Ring Notebook – Fill with pocketed dividers for a schedule organizer, project planner, or journal.

Dishwashing Tub – Use as a cubby for toys on shelves or the floor, store small tools in the garage, or hold craft supplies (especially tall bottles of glue or paint).

Plastic Coat Hanger – Organize belts for your closet, hang a mesh laundry bag on your bedroom door, or drape your uniform until it can be laundered again.

Plastic Milk Crate – Small crates make a great kid console for the backseat of your family's car, square-shaped ones store hanging files for projects or fundraising packs, and larger crates contain clutter on the go (videos, library books, and backpacks).

Wooden Peg Rack – Use as a towel rack for the bathroom, hat collection holder, a Tween Rack™ for clothes in your closet, or organize your backpack by the back door.

Canvas Book Bag – Utilize as a Grab-N-Go™ bag for outbound videos and library books, activity bag for traveling, or mail bag so that your notes from school don't get lost in the car or bus.

Over-the-Door Shoe Bag – Organize Beanie Babies® or Hot Wheels® cars, store your shoes off the closet floor, or transform into an arts and craft station.

Notes

Notes

Notes

Notes

Notes

Looking for a G-R-E-A-T Fundraising Opportunity?

Are your volunteers tired of selling the same old cookie dough or gift-wrap year after year? It's a proven fact among professional marketing strategists that books have a high-perceived value. Using *Organized Kidz* for your fundraising product can motivate your volunteers to share practical life skill resources while attracting new customers to your cause.

For each book that you sell, you keep HALF...that's a $7.50 profit for you!

What kinds of people benefit from using our books as fundraisers?

- Sports teams
- Private schools
- Gymnastic teams
- Cheerleaders
- Public schools
- Dance troupes
- Scouts
- Band Boosters
- Neighborhood Associations
- Women's Groups
- Youth Groups
- ... and many more!

By the Book Media books make **unique products** for your nonprofit group and practical products for your customers and their families. Why not get started on your fundraising campaign today? It's as simple as 1,2,3:

1. Download our user-friendly order form and distribute copies to your volunteers

2. Take orders and collect money from your customers

3. Turn in your order form with payment to By the Book Media.

We'll take care of the rest by shipping copies of *Organized Kidz* in 2-4 weeks to your fundraising leader along with a check for half of your collected funds (minus actual shipping costs).

Contact us Today for your Fundraising Solutions!
Email: info@organizedtimes.com
Phone: 281-286-9512

Give Your Family and Friends the Gift of ORGANIZATION!

AVAILABLE ONLINE AT
AMAZON.COM OR ORGANIZEDTIMES.COM

☐ **YES**, I want ___ copies of *Organized Kidz* at $14.95 each, plus $4 shipping (this applies only when ordering one or two books). For three or more books, please order online at organizedtimes.com. Allow 5-7 days delivery.

My check or money order for $ is _____ enclosed.

Name _____

Organization _____

Address _____

City/State/Zip _____

Phone _____ **E-mail** _____

Please make your check payable and return to:

By the Book Media
PO Box 590860
Houston, TX 77259

For credit card orders, please visit **Amazon.com** or **OrganizedTimes.com**

Give Your Family and Friends the Gift of ORGANIZATION!

AVAILABLE ONLINE AT
AMAZON.COM OR ORGANIZEDTIMES.COM

☐ **YES**, I want ___ copies of *Organized Kidz* at $14.95 each, plus $4 shipping (this applies only when ordering one or two books). For three or more books, please order online at organizedtimes.com. Allow 5-7 days delivery.

My check or money order for $ is _____ enclosed.

Name _____

Organization _____

Address _____

City/State/Zip _____

Phone _____ **E-mail** _____

Please make your check payable and return to:

By the Book Media
PO Box 590860
Houston, TX 77259

For credit card orders, please visit **Amazon.com** or **OrganizedTimes.com**

Printed in the United States
40403LVS00004B/27